EXTRAORDINARY BOSTON

1st Overleaf: Rowing shells, Charles River, Cambridge.   *2nd Overleaf:* Beacon Hill at dusk.

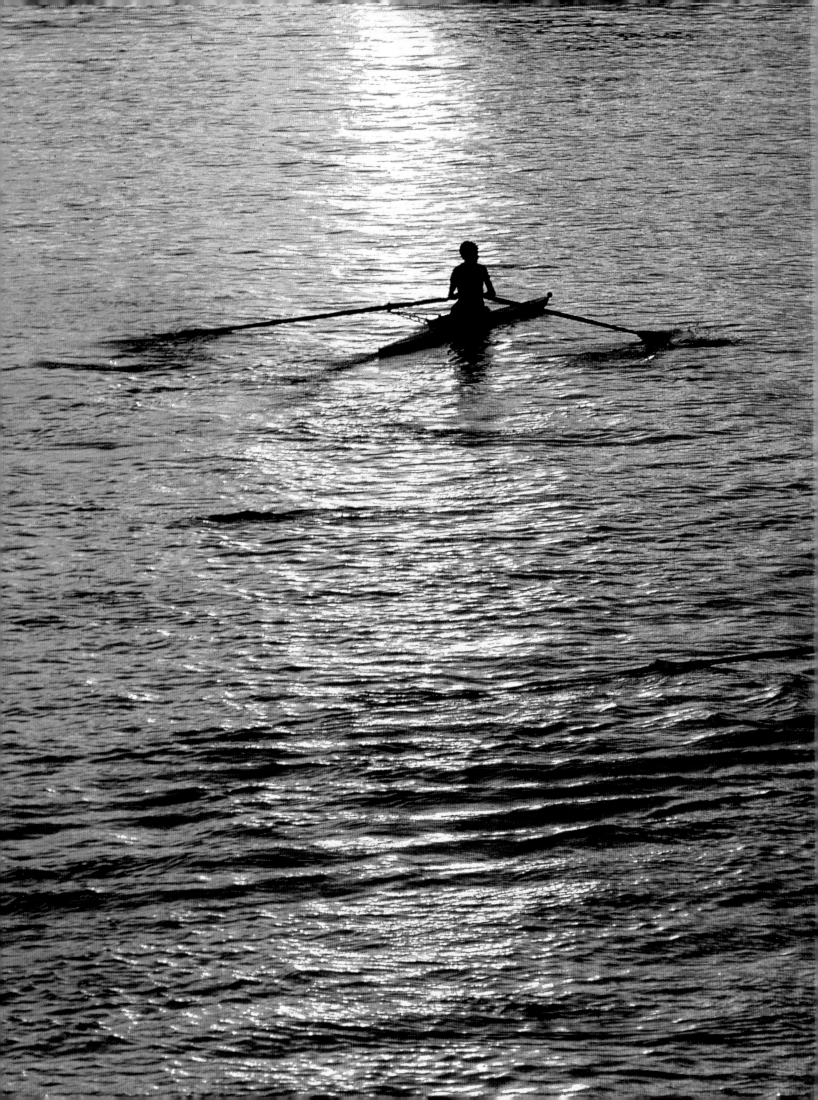

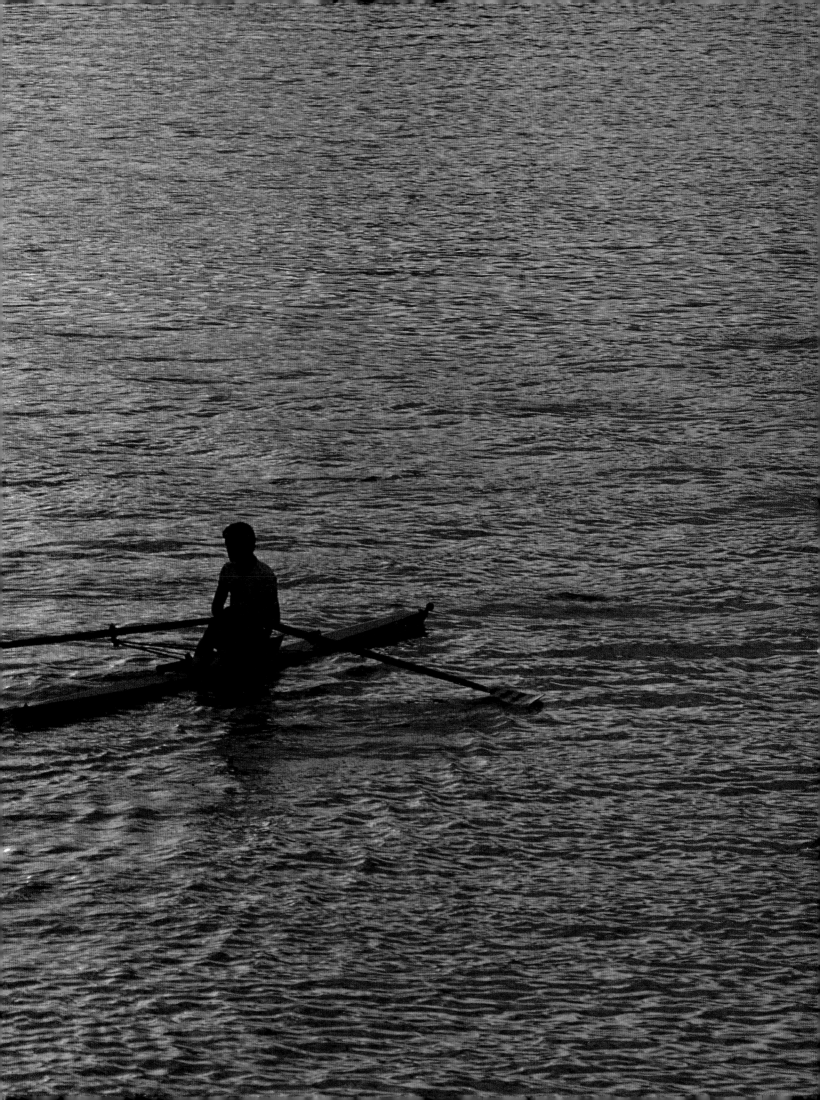

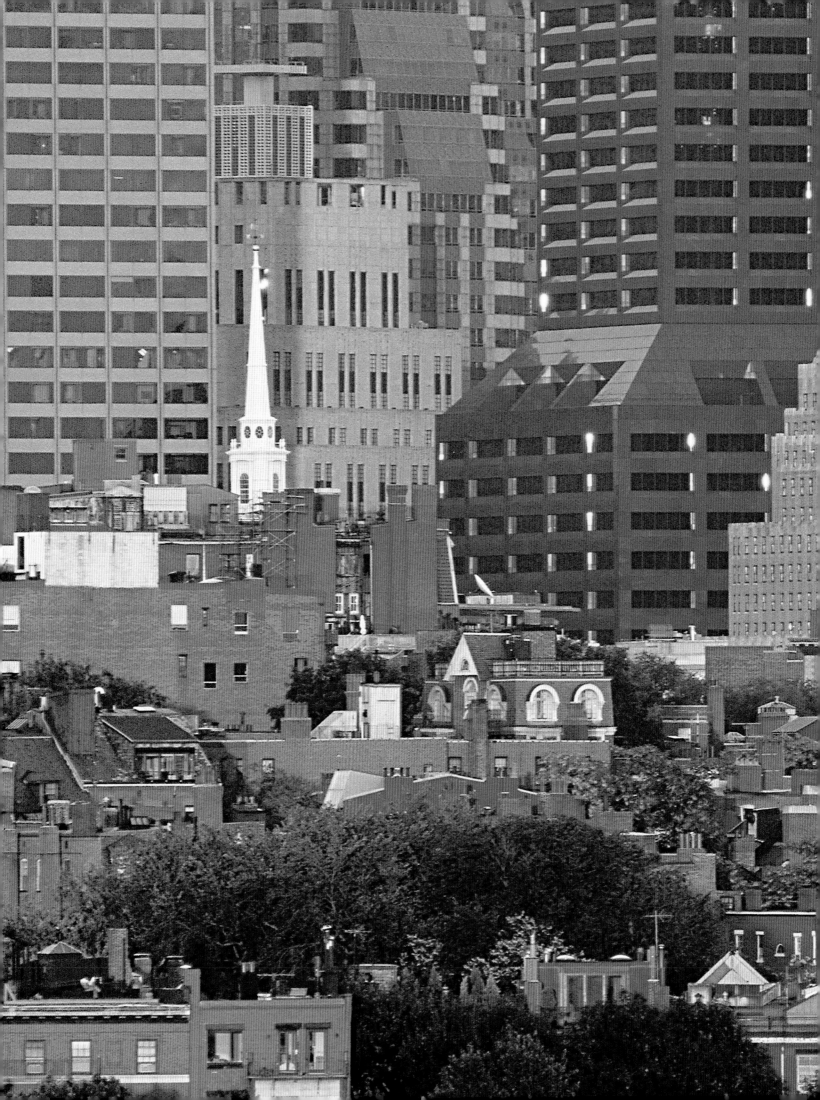

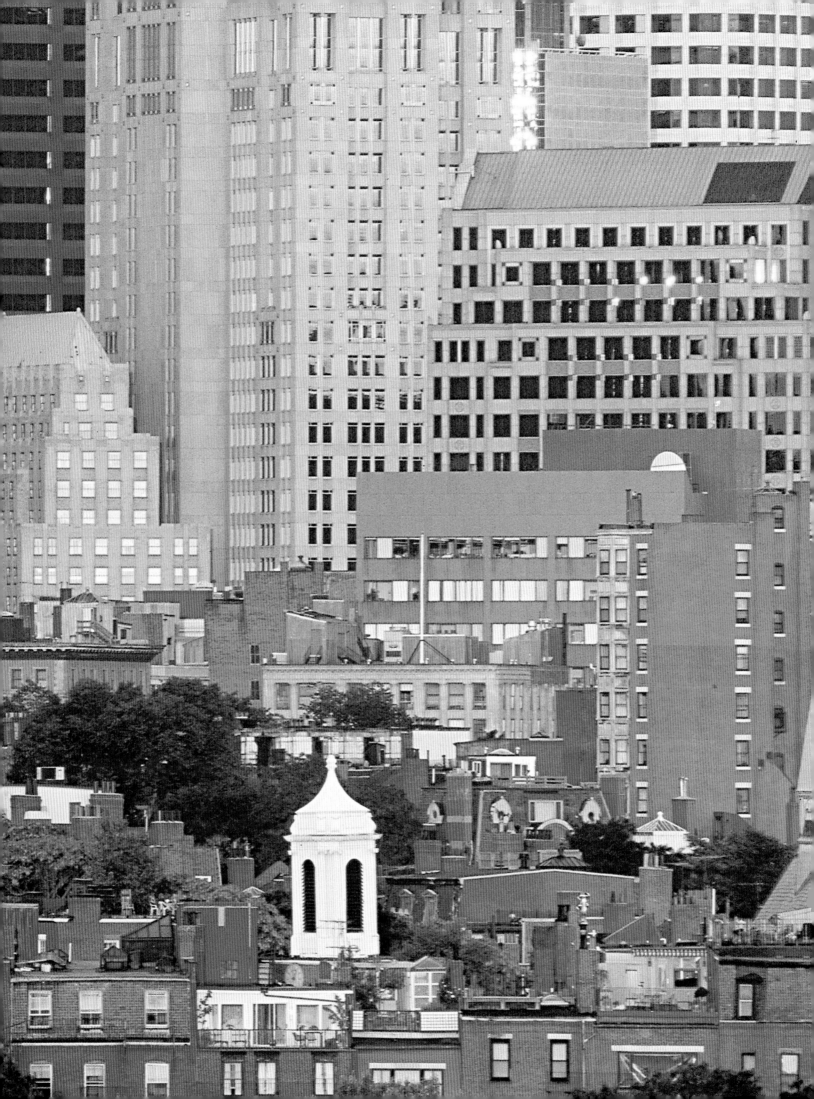

Edited by James Patrick.
Designed by Donald G. Paulhus.

Printed in China through Palace Press International

Library of Congress #94-79004

ISBN 0-9643015-0-4

Twelth Printing, 2003

Published by Back Bay Press
20 Winchester Street
Boston, MA 02116

EXTRAORDINARY BOSTON

Photography and text by Steve Dunwell

Published by Back Bay Press

EXTRAORDINARY BOSTON

This is a special place in America. Here, at the confluence of powerful natural, historical, commercial, and cultural currents, a unique metropolis has risen, sculpted by these forces and expressing their interplay. This is a city with resonance. Here the new is wrapped around and overlays the old without obscuring it, creating contrasts that enrich urban life, engage the mind and delight the eye. Transformed by imaginative and audacious enterprise, this city has become a dramatic metaphorical landscape. Modern towers challenge venerable monuments. Ancient enclaves persist within new districts. The Cradle of Liberty is ringed by the Nursery of Commerce and the Trade School of Architecture. Here the citizens of this narrow peninsula converted a good harbor into a great city: Extraordinary Boston.

Connoisseurs of Boston are the beneficiaries of this remarkable heritage. Every view reveals an aspect of transformation. Any walk through the city cuts across history like an archeological dig. Panoramas from roof tops or from the air provide new prospects on these juxtapositions. The higher the point of view, the more clearly the new encircles the old. The same sunlight which glances off cobbled streets and granite warehouses also blazes on the glass and chrome of adjacent towers, making an inspiring American landscape.

Early settlers used the Shawmut Peninsula much as they found it – setting a beacon on the highest hill, establishing their town on the flatland by the cove, and grazing their cattle on the Common. But this acceptance of natural limits was short-lived. Even before the Revolution, the waterfront was reshaped with wharves, dams, forts and seawalls. Two decades after Boston patriots tossed British tea into the harbor, Boston developers began shearing hilltops and dumping their gravel into the same harbor, starting a process of expansion and redefinition which has produced the city we see today.

Ambitious landfill became the theme of Boston development. Since the new buildings which colonized the new land used the latest styles, the expansion of the peninsula created a concentric history of architecture and urban design. Periodic fires and aggressive demolition wiped parts of the landscape clean, allowing new design to infiltrate the ancient Hub.

Charles Bulfinch set the tone for the city which expanded onto this altered landscape. He placed an elegant domed statehouse on John Hancock's hilltop pasture and designed stately symmetrical homes for the gentry on the slopes below. At General Hospital and along the wharves, his designs in granite are the acme of Federal style. At Quincy Market, his followers confirmed this early standard of excellence and imaginative design by superimposing long granite arcades on the run-down and ragged town docks that preceded it, creating a grand ceremonial entrance to the city from the harbor. More than just fine buildings, these designs establish urbane public spaces which characterize Boston.

From these auspicious beginnings, a parade of great architects and planners have designed new urban environments for the expanding city and superimposed them on the previous landscape. Louisburg Square was laid over the sheared hillside of Mt. Vernon. Ropewalks at the foot of the Common were cleared to make room for a grand Public Garden. The salt meadows of the Charles River were filled to make the South End, the Back Bay, and a new shoreline for Cambridge. On the dusty plain that became Copley Square, H. H. Richardson set his masterpiece – Trinity Church. F. L. Olmsted transformed the Muddy River swamps into the rustic Fenway and designed an Emerald Necklace for the remade peninsula.

The filled lands between the Public Garden and the Fenway became a showcase of Victorian style and energy. This was a prosperous and creative period for Boston. Lowell's power loom, Singer's sewing machine, Ames' ploughs and Gillette's razors made this a manufacturing center whose vitality continued even as the China Trade declined. Boston drew talent and invention like a magnet. Immigration brought new social pressure as the population doubled every decade. The citizens responded with a Grand Urban Experiment to transform the peninsula.

Now the Back Bay, the South End, and parts of downtown rebuilt after the Great Fire of 1872 are treasuries of architecture – on a grand scale and in ornamental detail. Richly articulated bay- and bow-fronts ripple down long axial streets. Mansard roofs of myriad patterns provide a rich and varied crest to the sturdy brick blocks which march west from the Common. South End streets are relieved by quiet oval inlets at Union Park, Worcester Square and Chester Square.

The treasury of Boston buildings offers a world tour without leaving the peninsula. A Florentine campanile marks the skyline along with English church steeples. Replicas of a Petrograd bridge, a Venetian palazzo, and a French boulevard enliven the landscape. Every district has its Greek temple. Egyptian lotus columns grace selected entries. Exuberant stylistic vitality enriches the city. The South End has its Cyclorama; Back Bay, its Second Empire mansions. Teutonic castles guard the entrances to India Street and to Columbus Avenue. Tiled pyramids top off skyscraper ziggurats. Allegorical figures and historical bas-relief educate the pedestrian about the cultivation of tea, the principles of navigation and the virtue of Industry.

By the turn of the century the transformation was almost complete. Between the Institute of Technology on the north and the Esplanade on the south, the Charles River became – at high tide – a reflecting pool for Beacon Hill. The waterfront expanded until its radius equalled Long Wharf. Similar wharfing-out converted Noddles Island into East Boston and Dorchester Heights into South Boston. Warehouses and manufacturing lofts surrounded the vestiges of Fort Point Channel. Radiating from the Hub, the streetcar suburbs of Jamaica Plain, Brookline, Brighton, and Roxbury were relieved by Olmsted's Emerald Necklace of parkland, ending – in concept – at Castle Island, now joined to Southie at the tip of Marine Park. Citizens of Boston admired the trees of the Arnold

Arboretum and strolled the pastures of Franklin Park.

During this century of expansion, the Boston skyline was marked mainly by church spires and chimneys. The most dramatic vertical accents were the granite obelisk atop Bunker Hill, the eagle-topped shaft Bulfinch placed on Beacon Hill, and Boston Light. Standing beside the Old State House, the thirteen-story Ames Building was the city's tallest office block. The skyline kept this low profile until 1913, when a thirty-story Art Deco tower was planted above the rotunda of the Customs House. This dramatic landmark ruled the skyline for a half-century, setting a new standard for audacity in design – the new right on top of the old – that previewed the great skyscrapers which followed. Over the freight yards of the Back Bay, Prudential created a new family of towers. Beside venerable Trinity Church, Hancock angled a monumental glass obelisk. Scollay Square was erased to make room for Government Center. Copley Place vaulted over the turn-pike corridor. Only two blocks from the Customs House, Exchange Place updates the concept with blue glass walls soaring over the old granite facade. At nearby Fort Hill, International Place rises where both fort and hill have vanished.

The new glass and steel towers have transformed the Boston skyline as forcefully as the preceding landfill remade its perimeter. Confined by a High Spine concept, separated from sacred residential districts, these sky-scrapers march in an articulated column from the Fens to the Hub, massing there in a concentrated upthrust of commercial energy – a simplified meta-phorical promenade of enterprise approximating the original peninsula.

With its spine of new towers, Boston packs dense urban culture into a small place. Walking from the edge of the Fens to the tip of Long Wharf takes only an hour, yet covers three centuries of civic invention. Indeed, among the great delights of Boston is the miniaturization which local geography has enforced. The transformed and layered cityscape is chal-lenging, yet comprehensible. It is small enough to know, yet rich enough to reward continuing study. Though packed with skyscrapers, the Hub is still only minutes from the Common and the harbor. Any random stroll samples many diverse environments.

This is a city which rewards the pedestrian. The citizen can perambulate the Hub, study its variegated texture, and contemplate its history. Walking through Boston, one can sense more easily the spirit of the intellectual giants who occupied the Hub before the corporate towers muscled in. Daniel Webster and Horace Mann guard the State House. Park Street Church still echoes with Garrison's abolitionist zeal. Emerson, Longfellow and Whittier can be imagined on the streets of Beacon Hill.

From high-rise offices, the citizen can survey broad panoramas. The exercise of imagination and the limits of creativity become clear. Only the aviator sees more. Viewed from above, Boston reveals its transformed topography. As altitude increases, the outlines of the peninsula and the harbor emerge. Architecture recedes into texture as the developer's hand clearly dominates. Historical relationships between Boston, Charlestown, Dorchester and Cambridge become visible. At the highest altitudes, the encircling arms of Cape Ann and Cape Cod come into view, dramatizing the shelter and opportunity which distinguish Boston Harbor.

Like the obelisks of Stonehenge, the towers of the Hub and the grid behind it record the changing seasons and shifting angles of light. The Bunker Hill monument serves as a giant sundial for Charlestown. Radial avenues dramatize the solar calendar. Watch the summer sun as it lights the Old State House at dawn and turns Summer Street warehouses to dusky gold. Behold Commonwealth Avenue in October as the setting sun shoots along its rippling facades. See the harvest moon float up over Beacon Hill. Winter sunsets transfigure South End avenues. At Copley Square, the Hancock Tower reflects and intensifies both light and weather while measuring the days with its shadow. As spring approaches, a celebration of magnolia blossoms surprises the Back Bay. The city comes alive with dramatic light.

The views collected here distill the impressions of a Boston enthusiast. First as a visitor, then as a resident, I have learned the resonance of this special city. These images preserve the wonders of discovery that make learning fun. It's only a short walk from my door to the Public Garden, and as I turn onto Arlington Street, I sense the marshy tide flat that it used to be. The brick sidewalk even seems a bit more springy. Arriving at the Garden, I marvel now as I did when I first saw it – an oasis in this brick enclave, graced by stately swanboats. Standing between the Doric columns of the Custom House, I can see the bowsprits of clipper ships moored in front and imagine Hawthorne hunched over his ledger inside. Climbing Copps Hill, I look across to Charlestown and see Paul Revere waiting.

Photographs can freeze special moments and angles where all elements are optimized. Too often the view flashes by, as the city seems to do when seen from commercial aircraft on take-off or landing. Before the traveler can say "Look at the light on that building!" the moment is gone. These photographs intend to capture some of those fleeting glimpses and crystallize them for future study. Through views of the city we understand better its underlying principles.

Boston is a taut web of urban vitality. Unique among American cities, it has the range and depth of history on display. Lines of influence link Old North Church to Bunker Hill, Old Ironsides to Boston Lighthouse. Commercial energy crackles between the Customs House Tower and the Hancock Tower. The quest for enlightenment joins the spires of Park Street to Harvard Square. Bronson Alcott described this as a city "upon which the light of the sun of righteousness has risen." To our amazement, his claim was not entirely arrogant. Boston is, indeed, illuminated by a special light. As the sun clears the horizon by the nation's oldest lighthouse, it shines on a tiny gem of urban imagination set in a dramatic harbor of history. Poignant and hopeful, the Hub glows in the dawn.

Steve Dunwell
Boston, Mass.

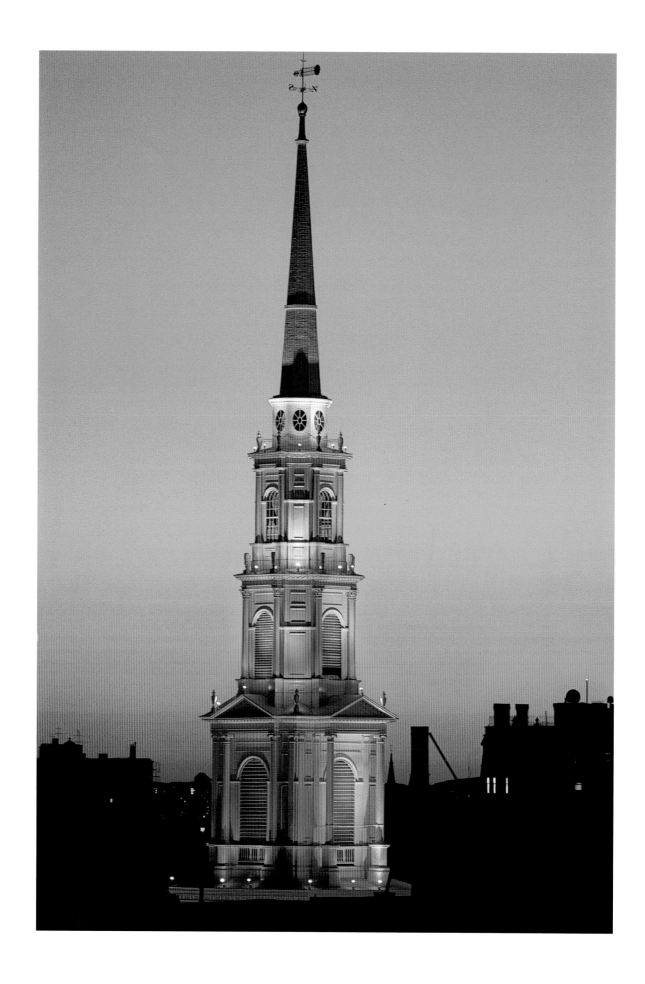

Park Street Church, 1809 Spire   Beacon Hill

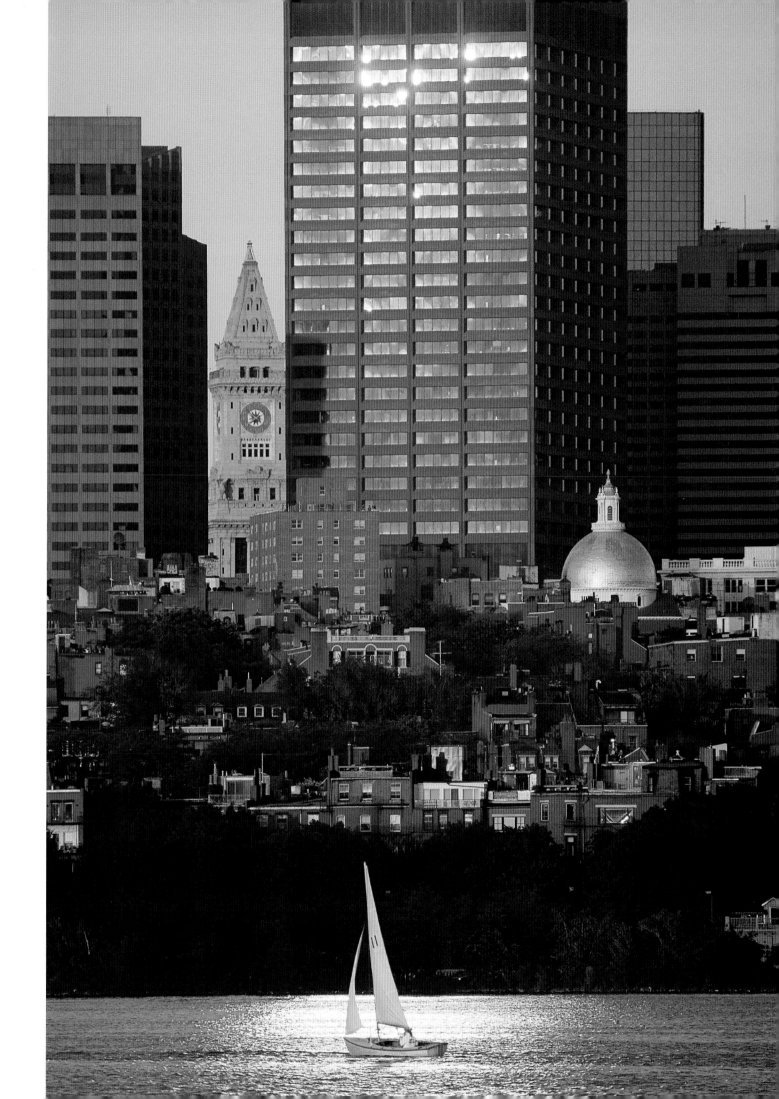

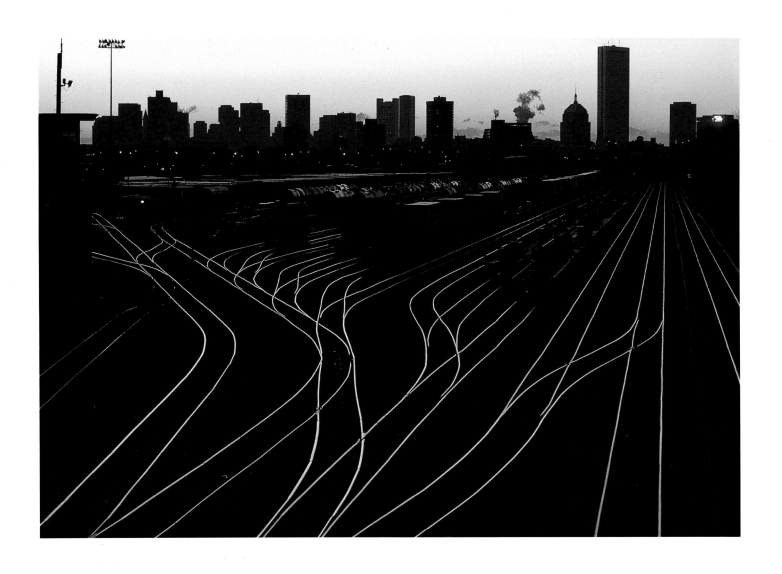

Freight yard skyline, Allston

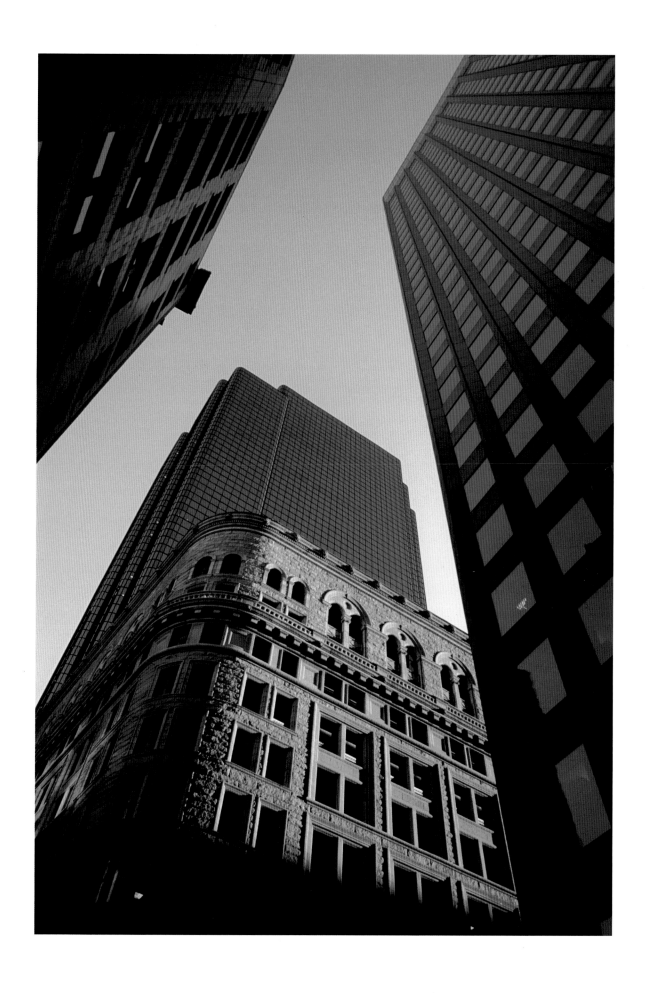

Old Stock Exchange, State Street

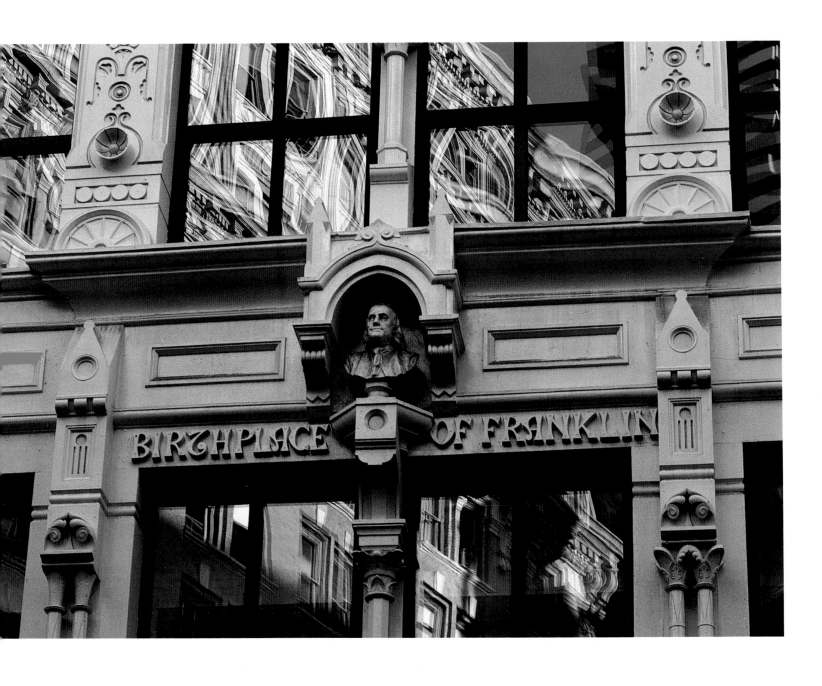

Boston Post Building, Milk Street

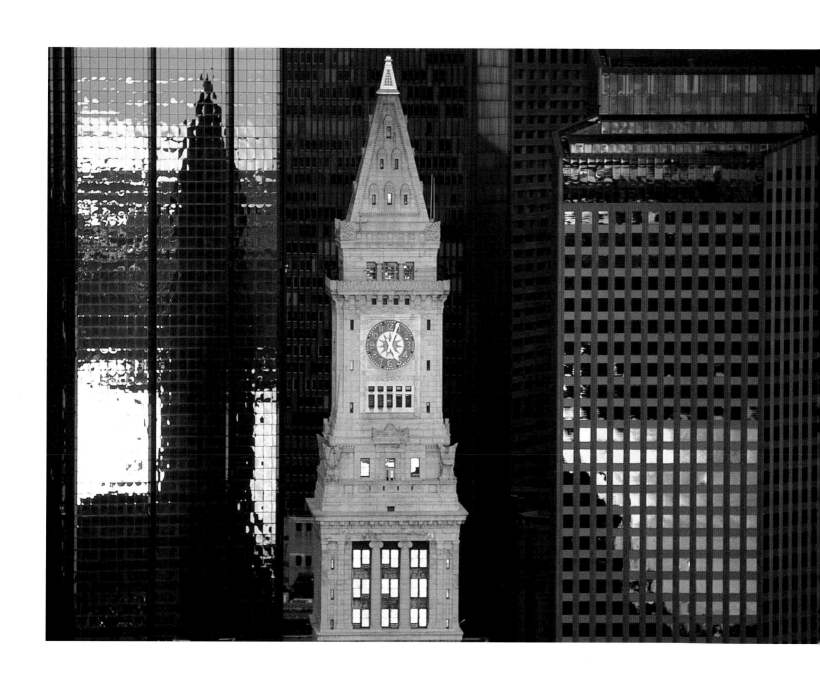

Customs House tower, State Street

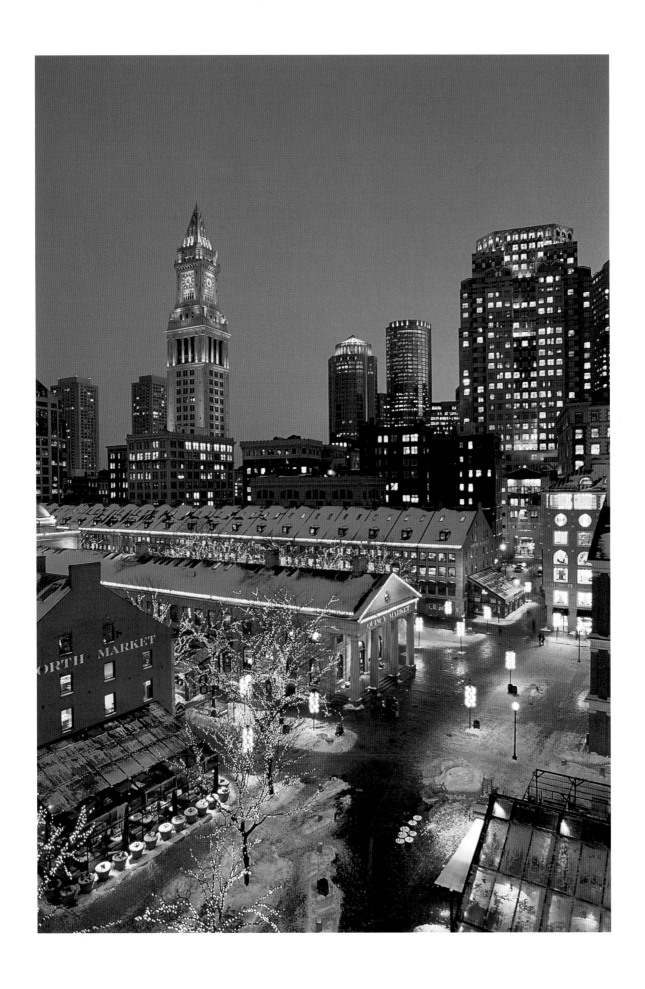

Quincy Market, Customs House Tower

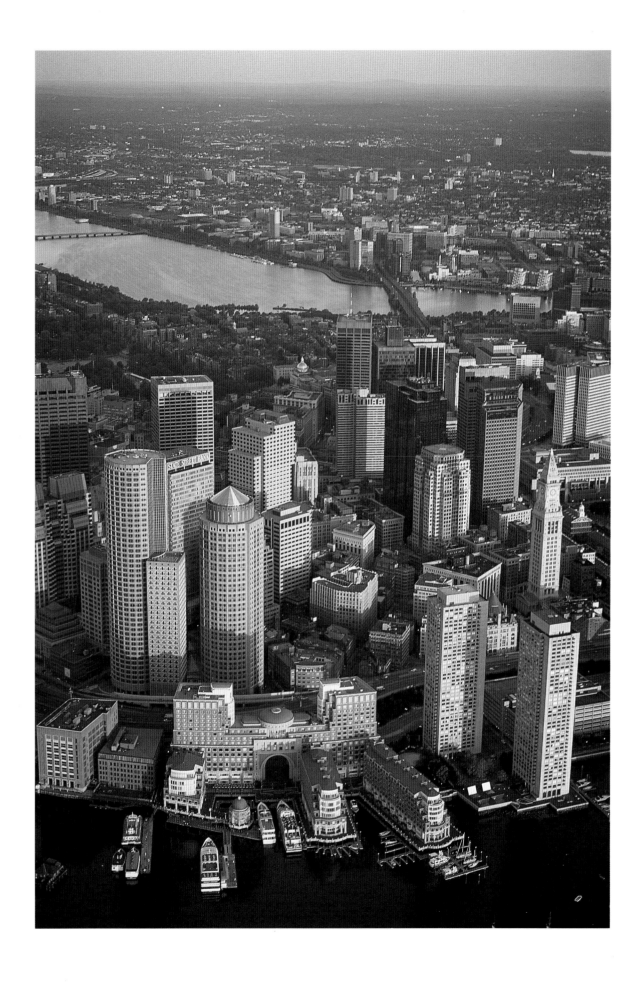

Rowes Wharf, financial district   *Overleaf:* USS Constitution

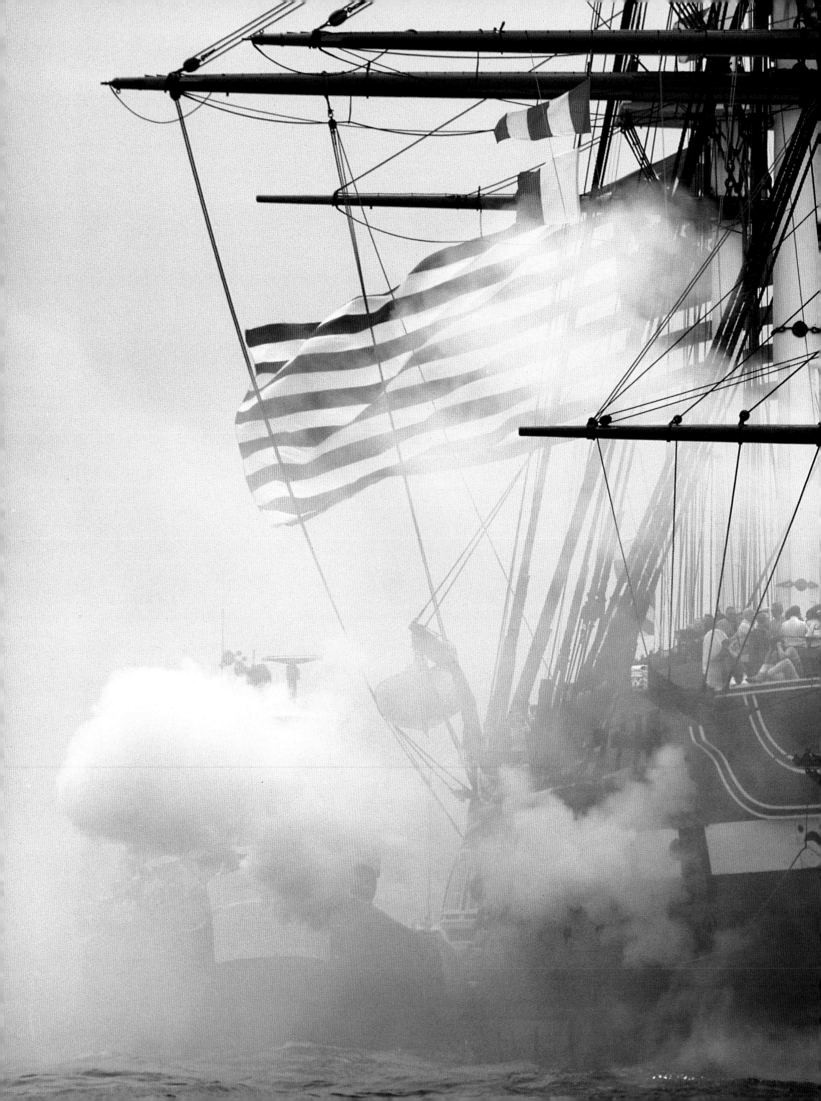

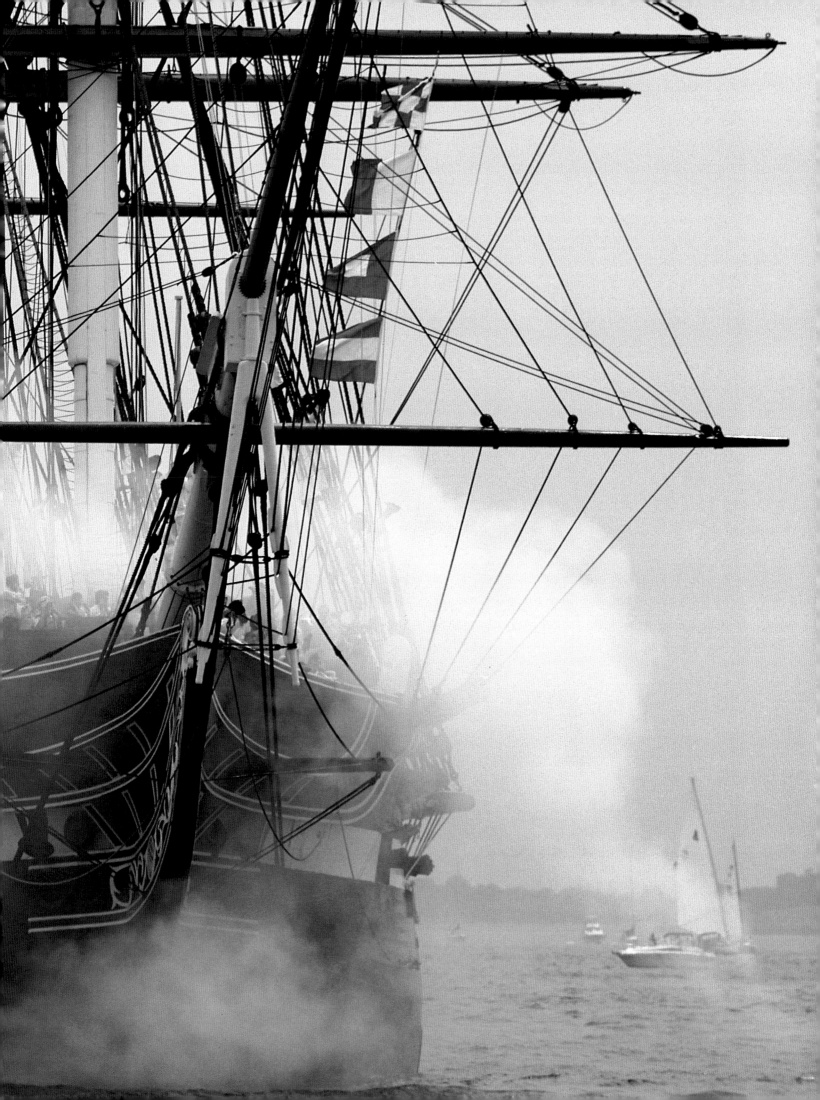

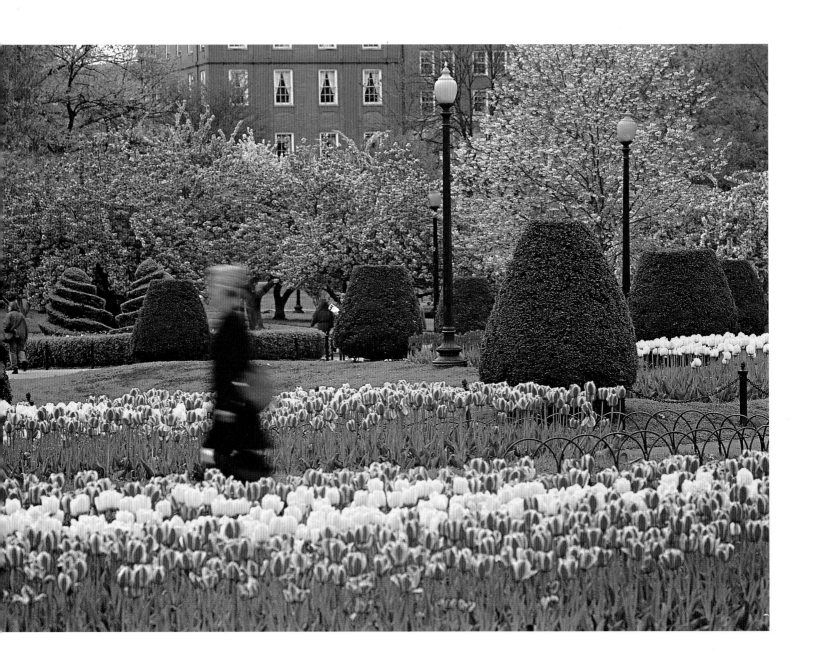

Spring afternoon, Public Garden　　　Victorian swanboats, Public Garden

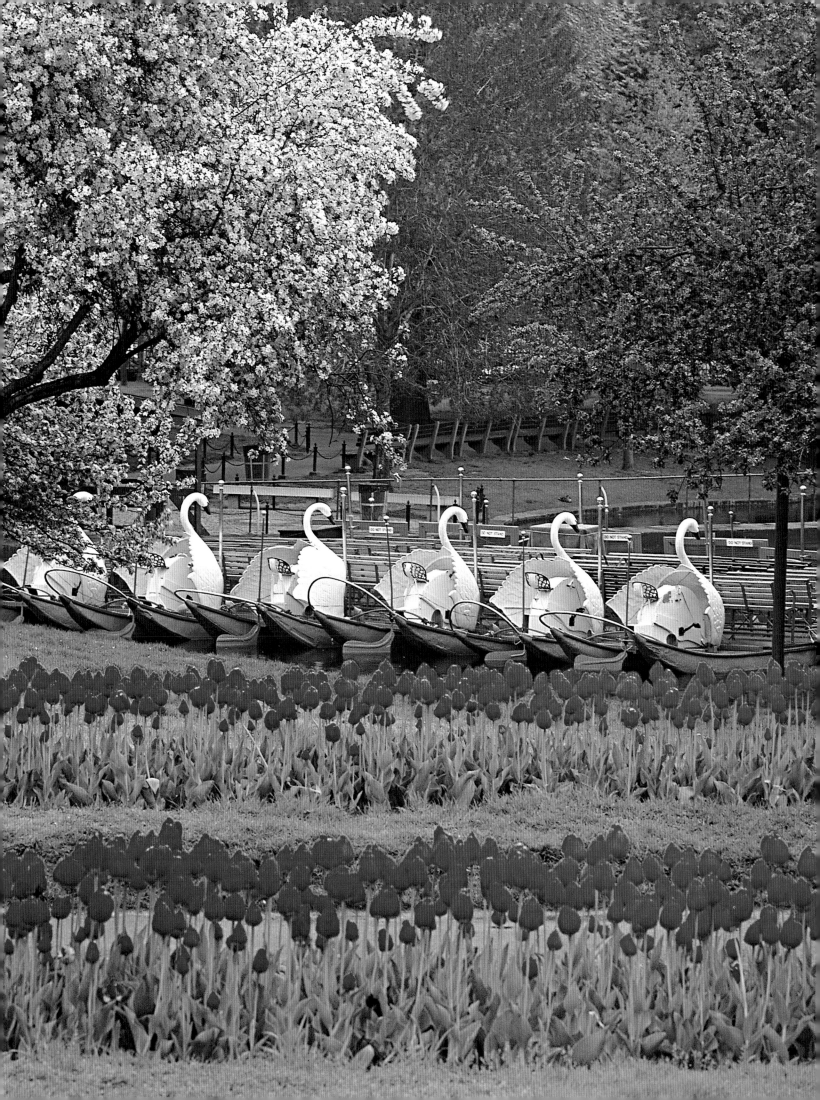

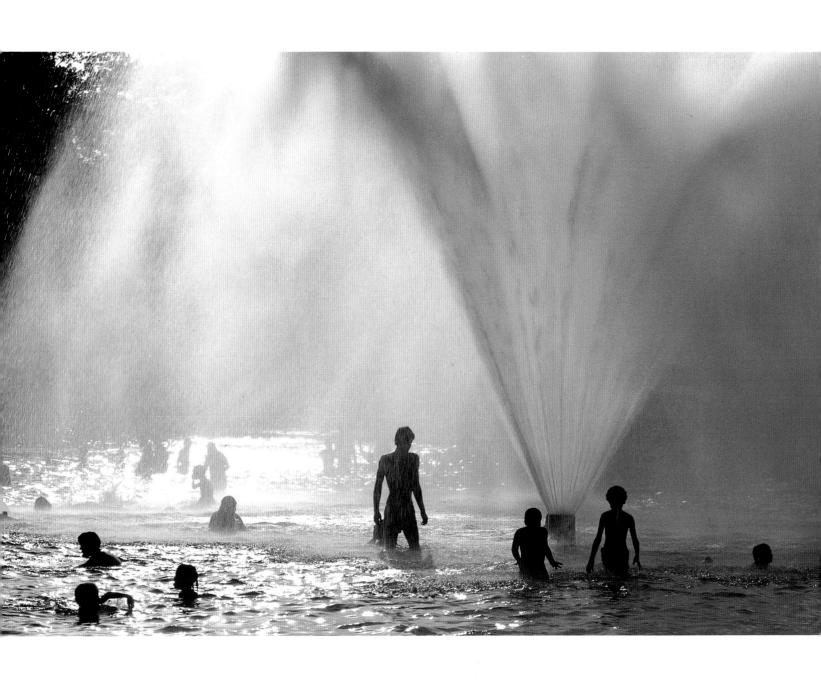

Frog Pond fountain, the Common

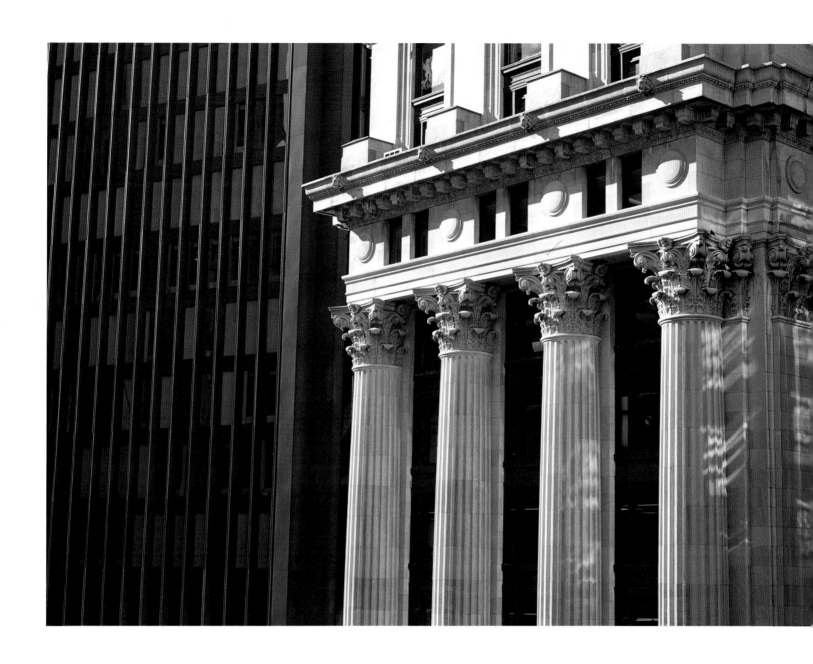

Corinthian columns, State Street   *Overleaf:* Beacon Hill skyline, Boston University boathouse

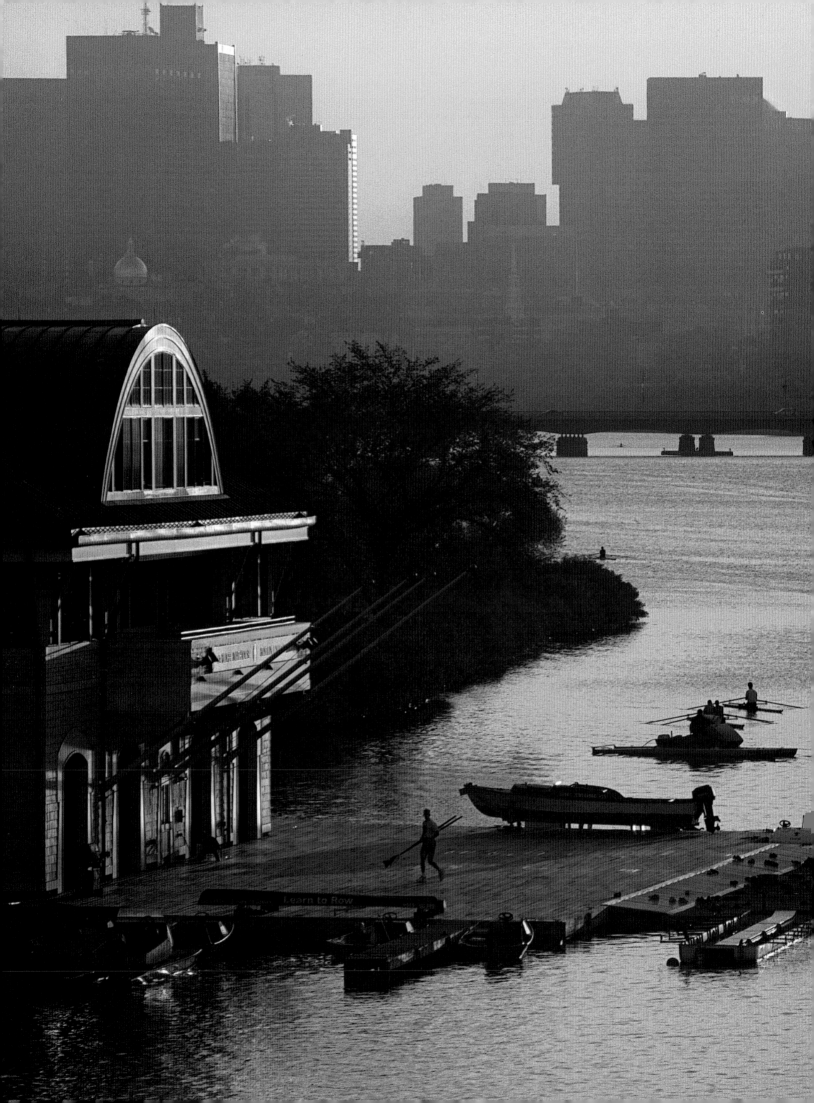

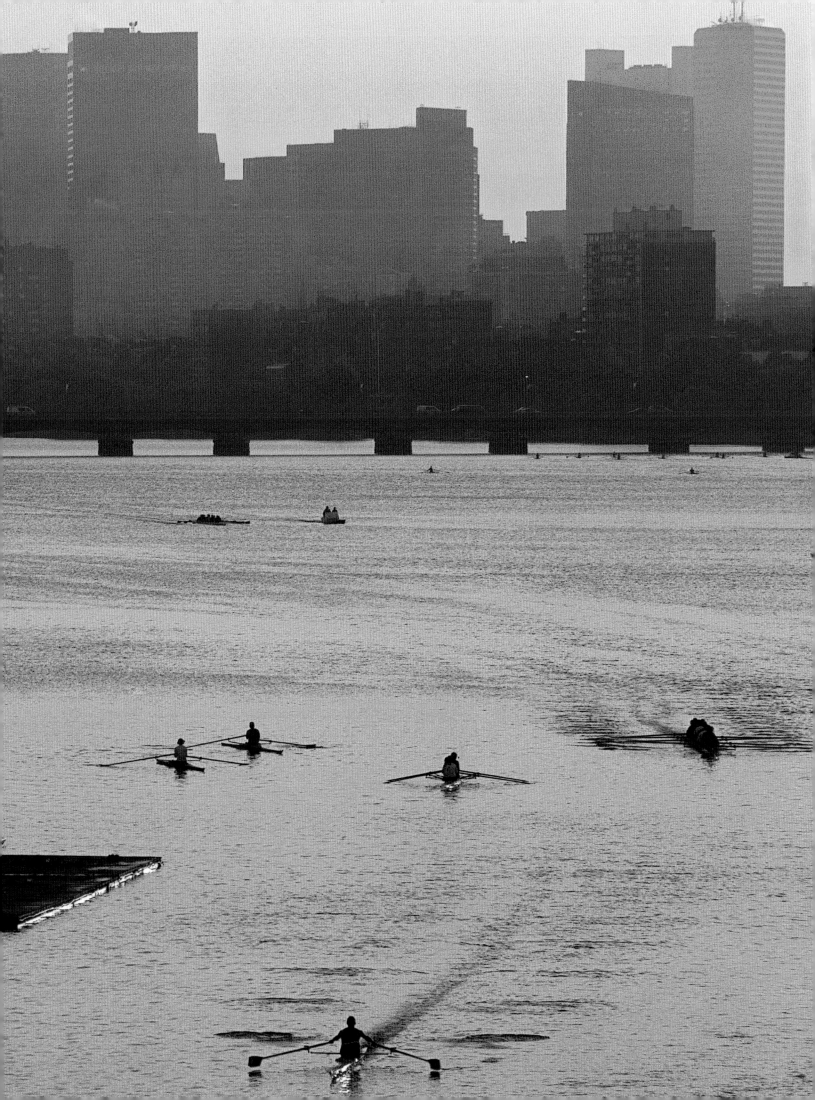

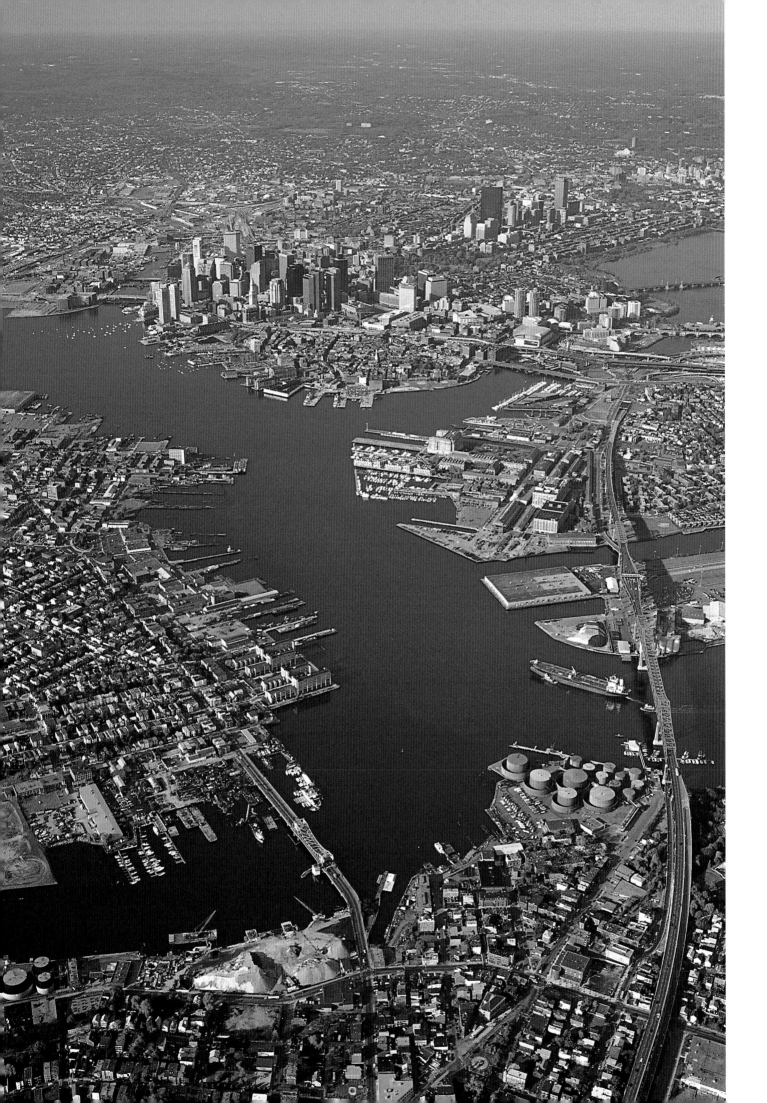

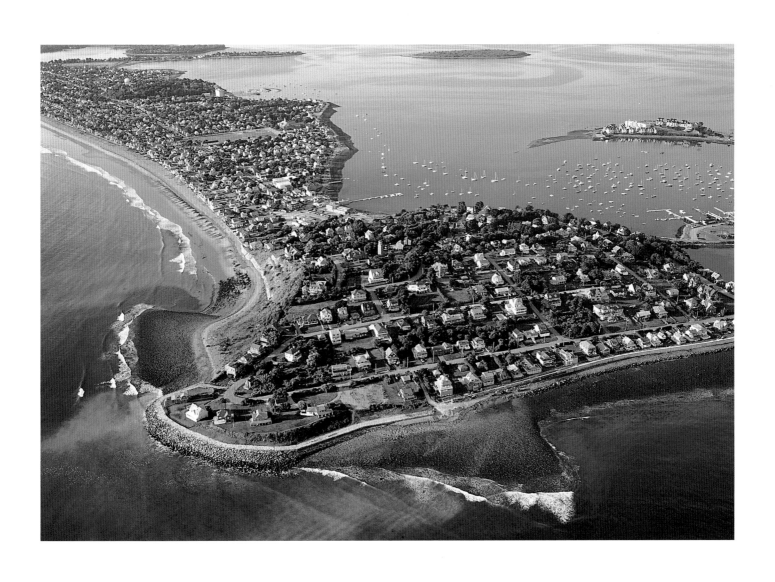

Inner harbor, East Boston

Nantasket peninsula, Hull

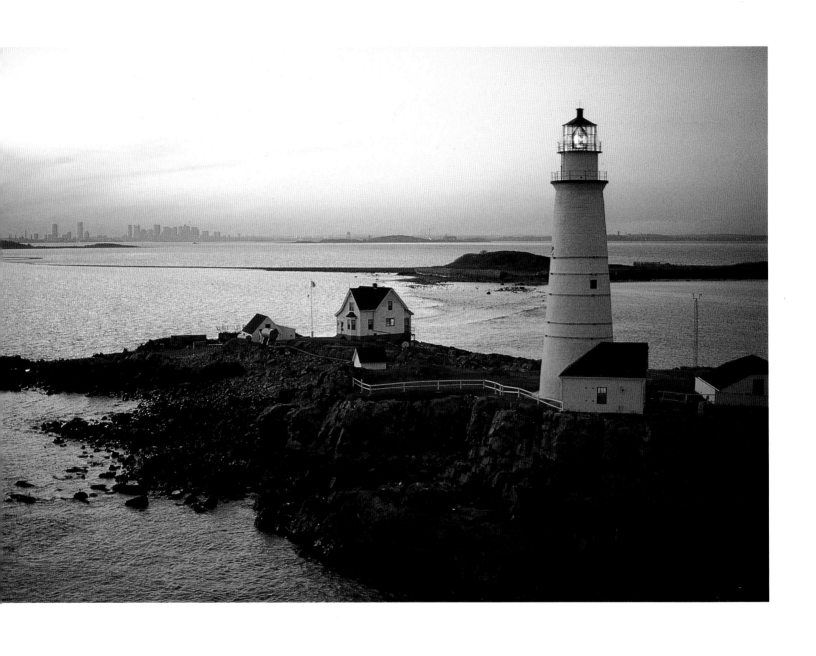

Boston Light, Little Brewster Island

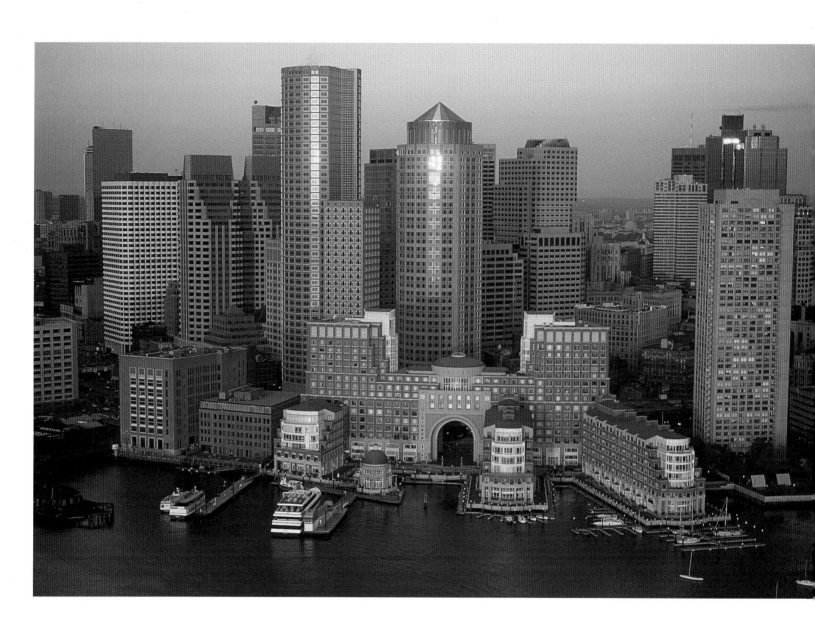

Boston Harbor, sunrise

Overleaf: Bandstand, Crescent Beach, Revere

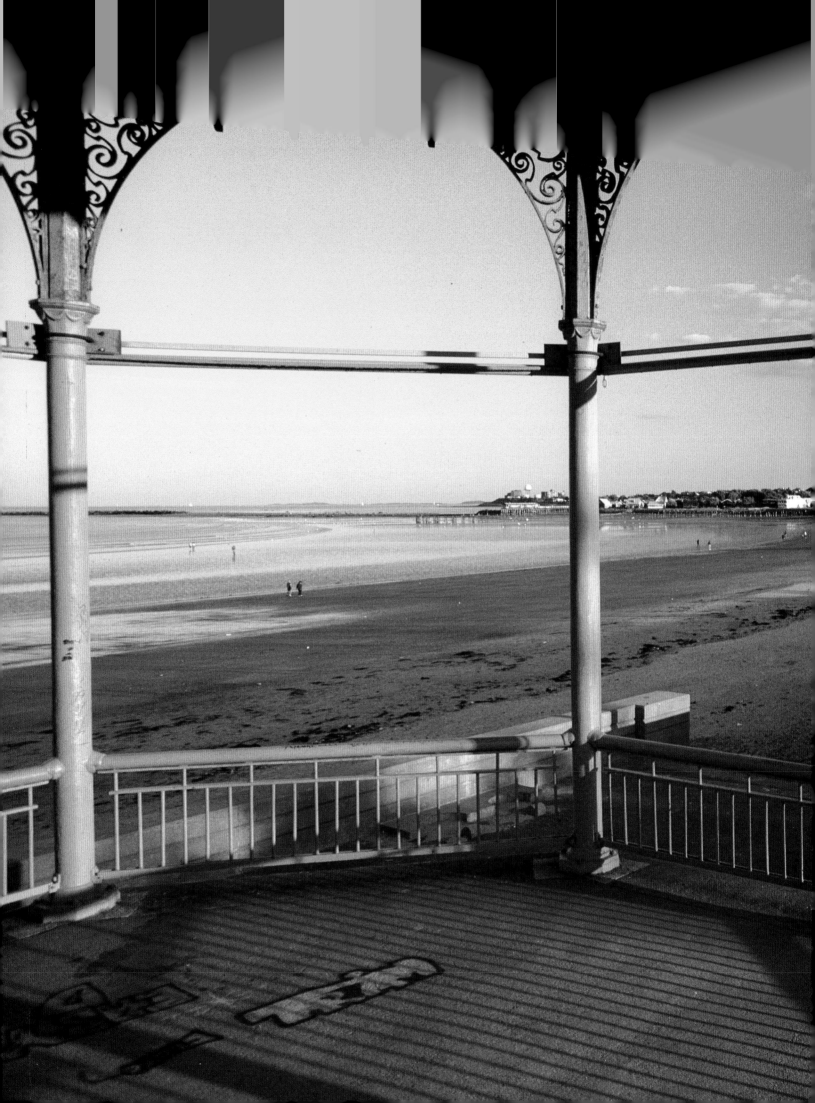

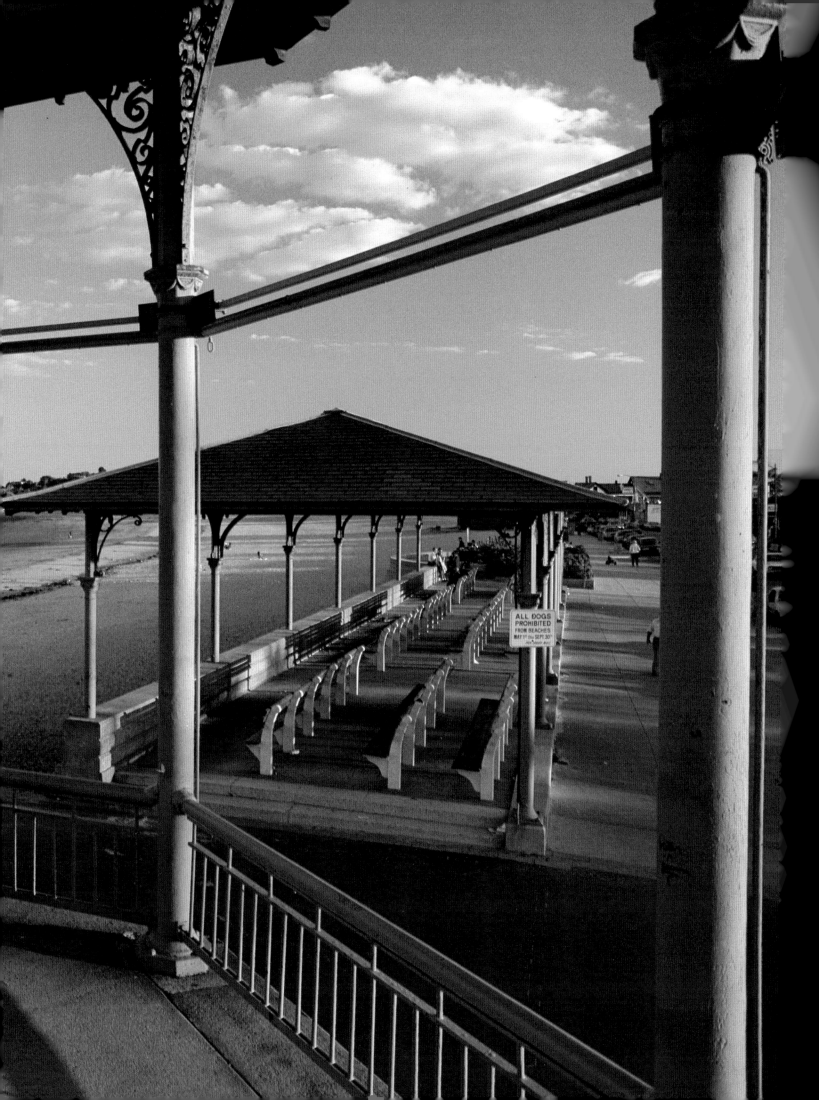

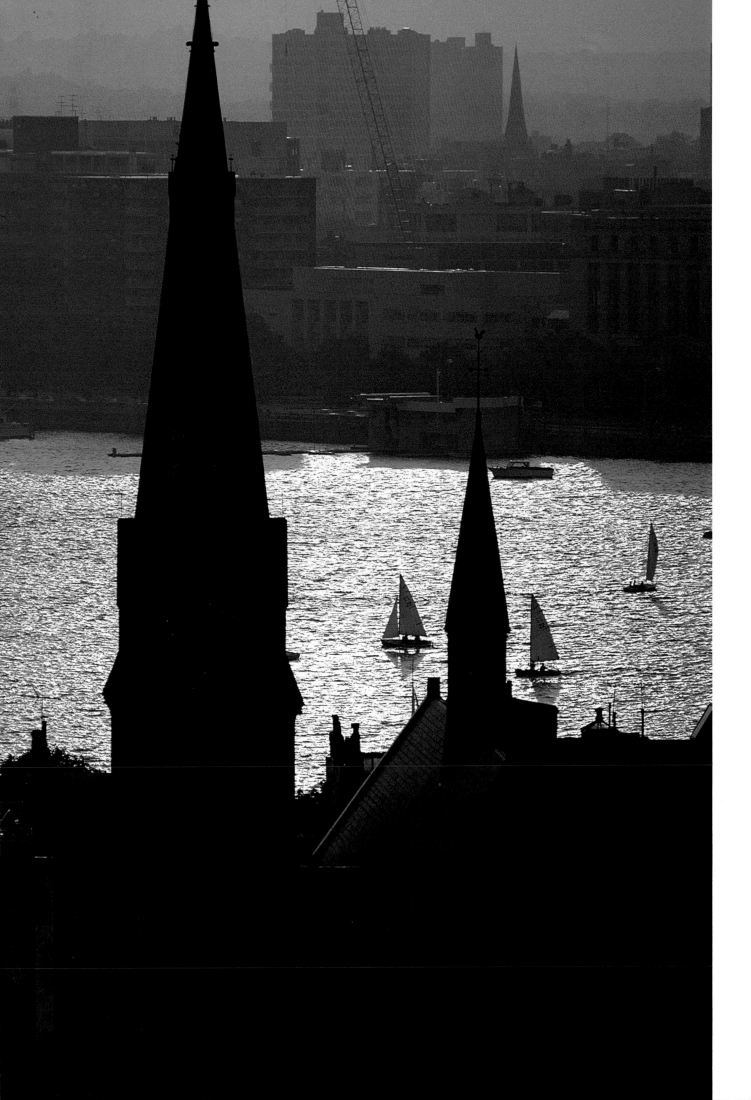

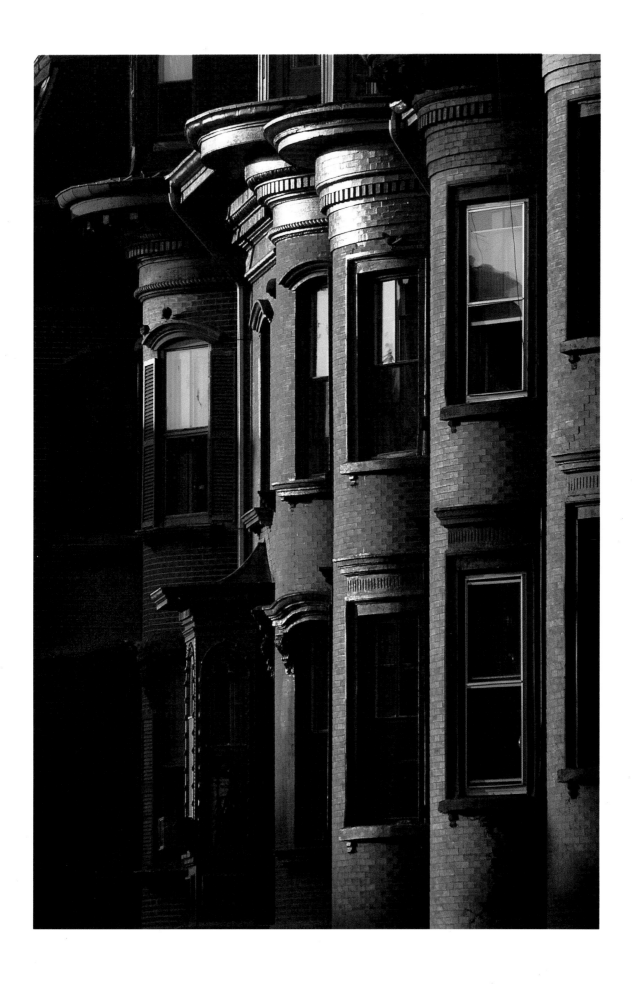

Church of the Advent, view towards Cambridge   Chester Square bowfronts, South End   35

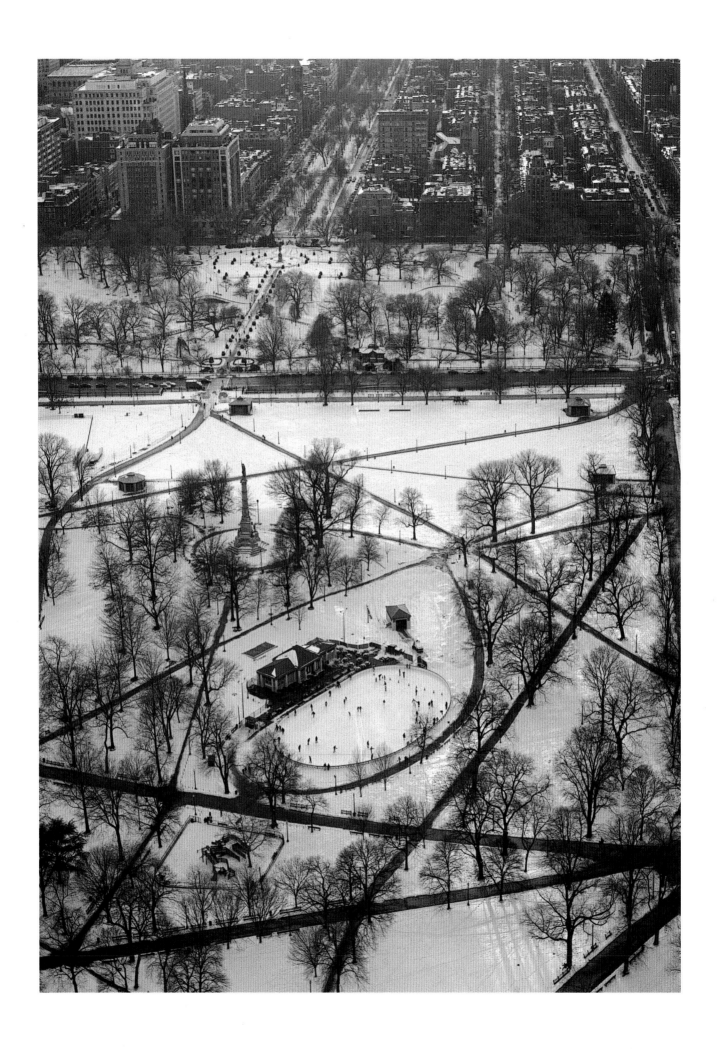

Boston Common, towards Back Bay

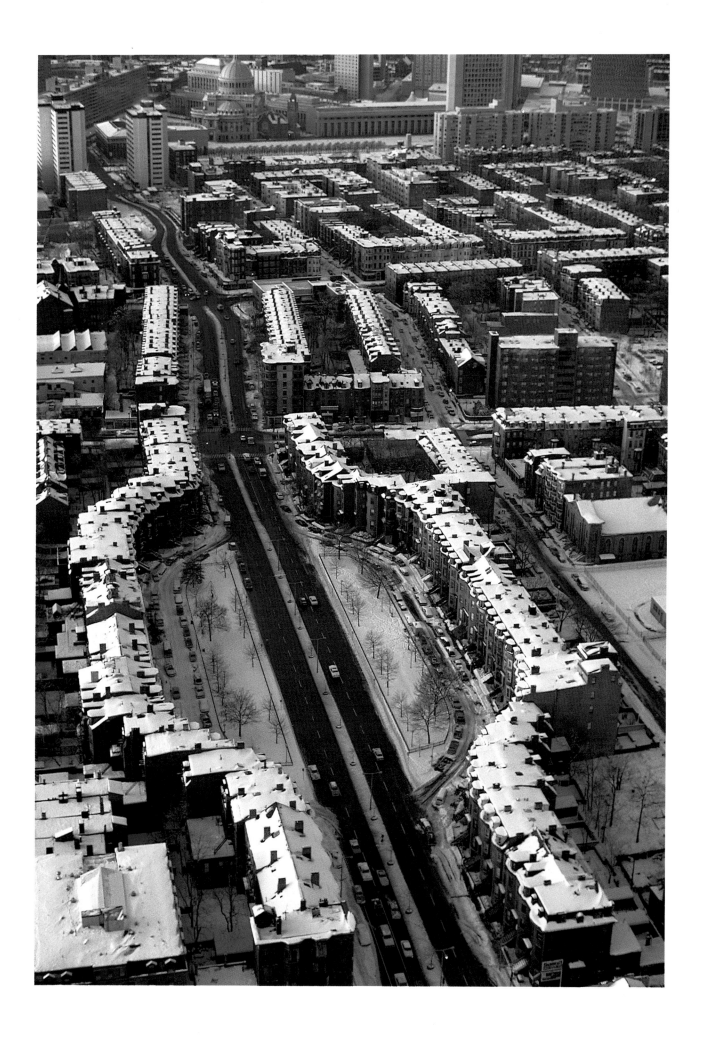

Chester Square, Massachusetts Avenue

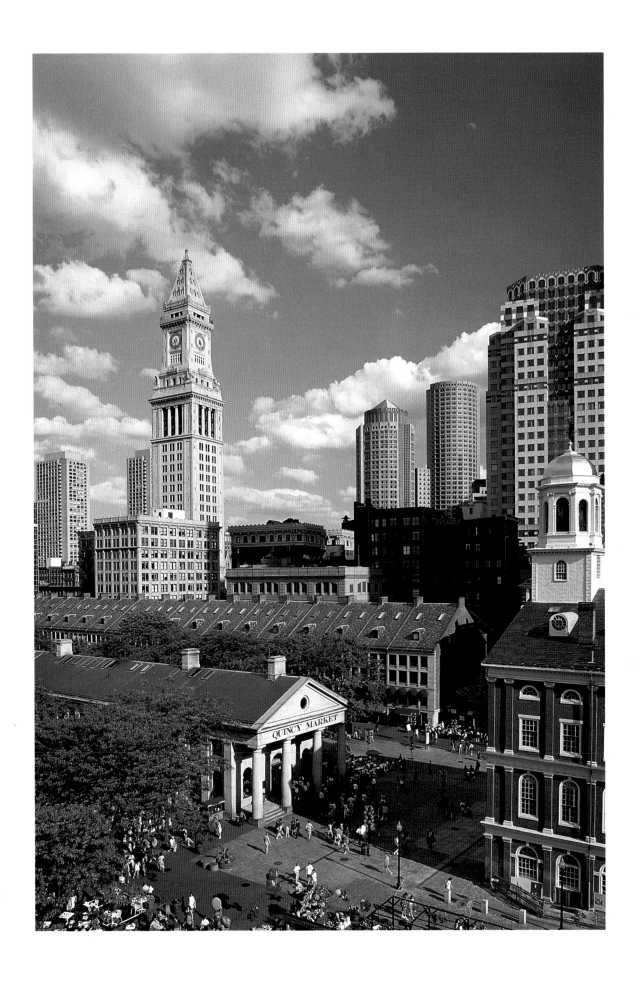

Faneuil Hall, Quincy Market

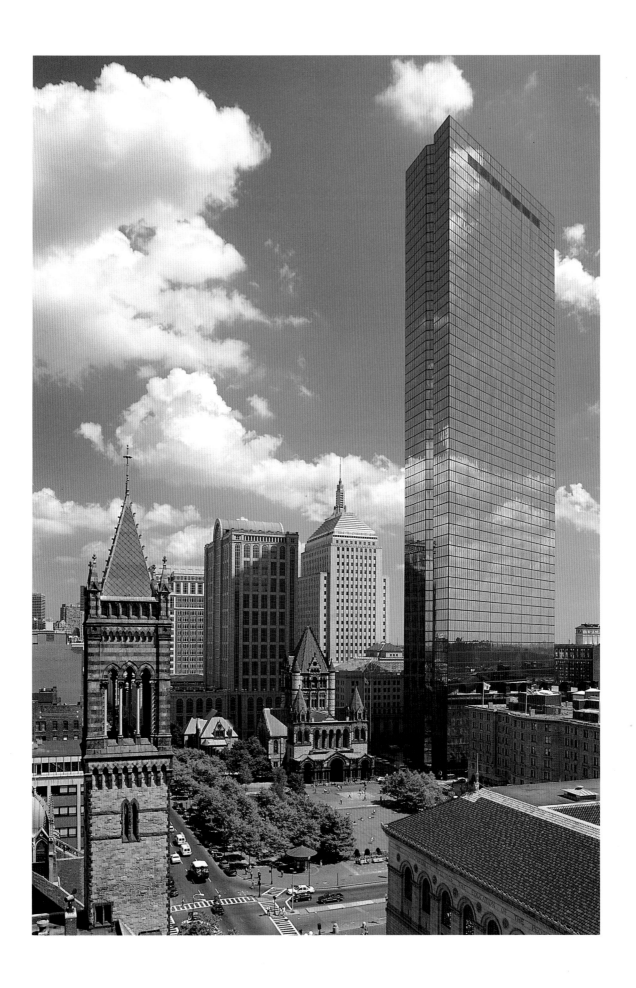

Old South and Trinity Church, Copley Square

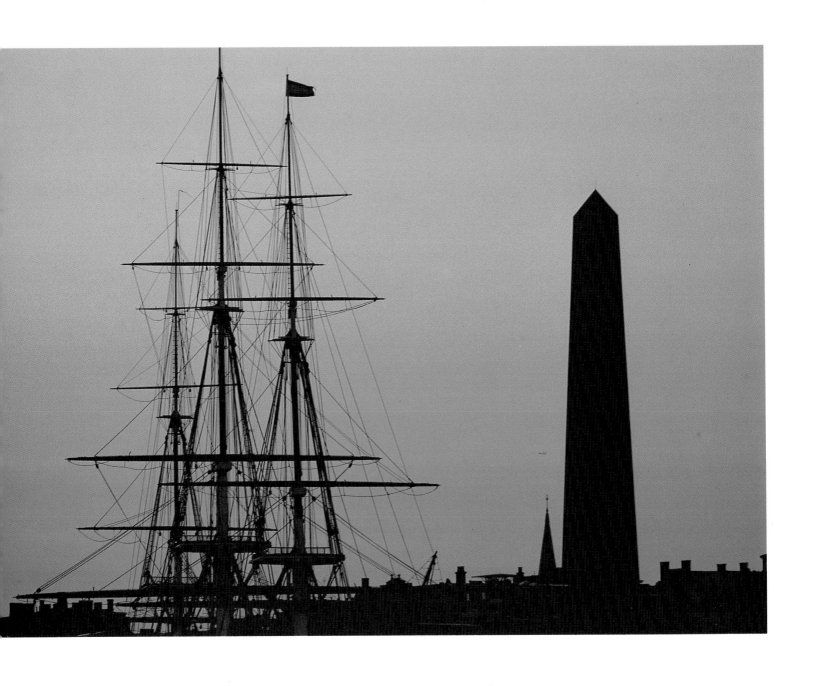

U.S.S. Constitution rigging, Bunker Hill, Charlestown

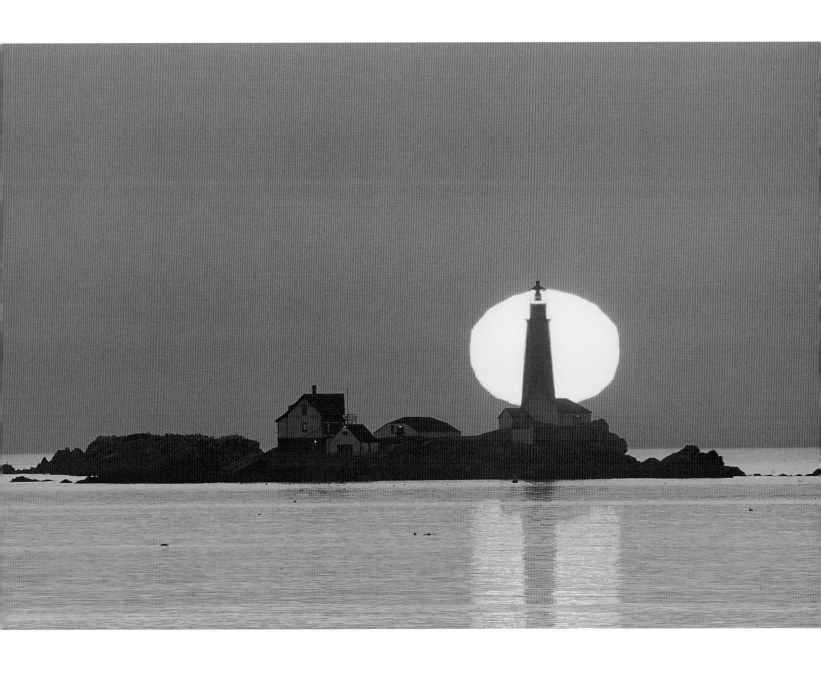

Boston Lighthouse

Overleaf: Zakim Bridge

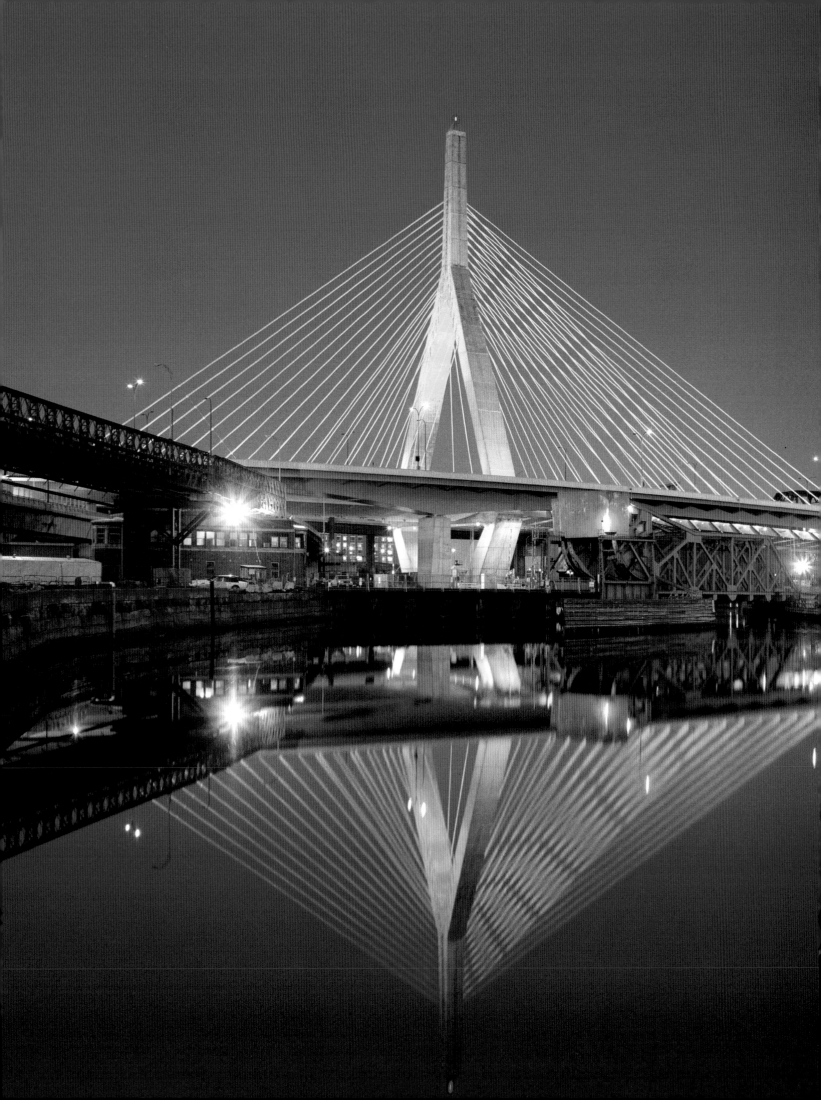

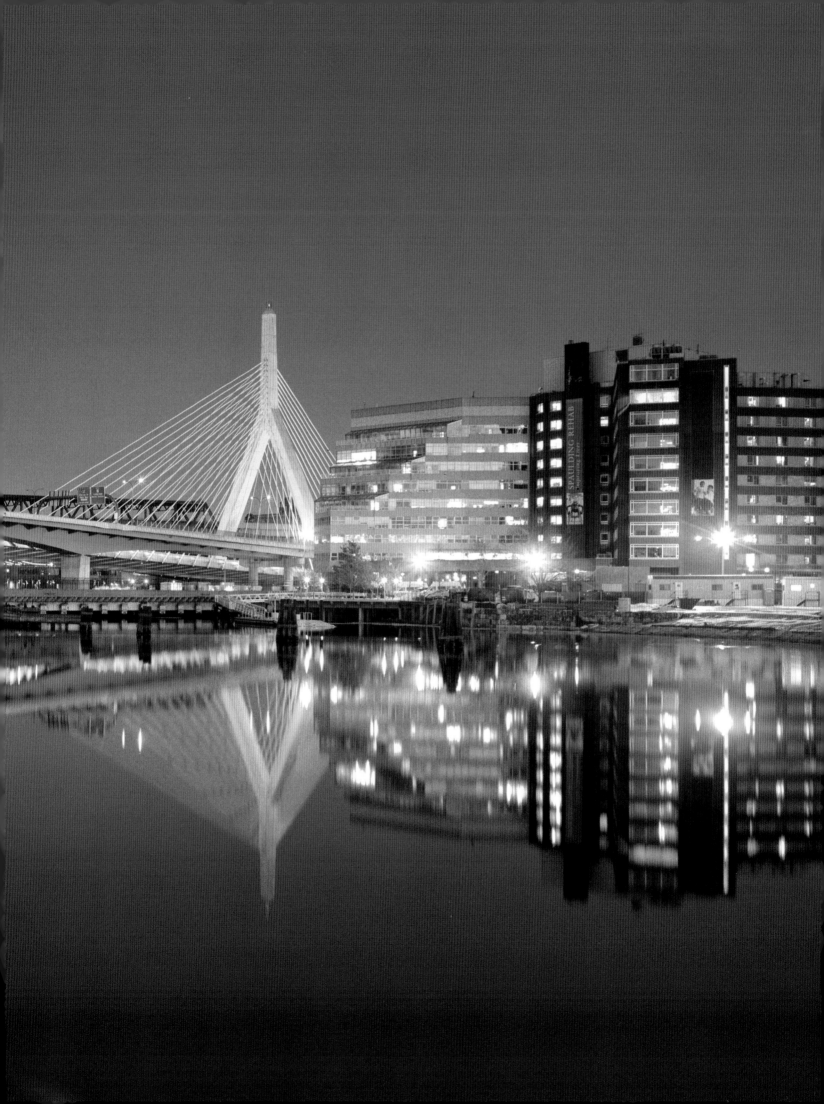

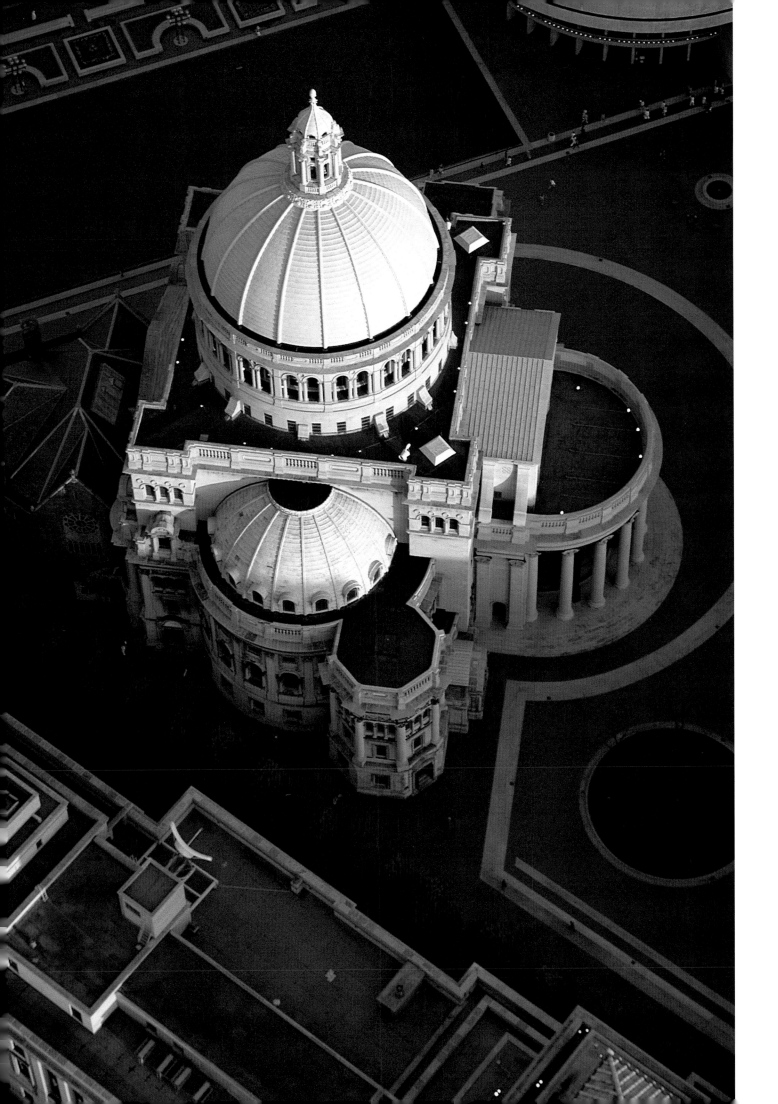

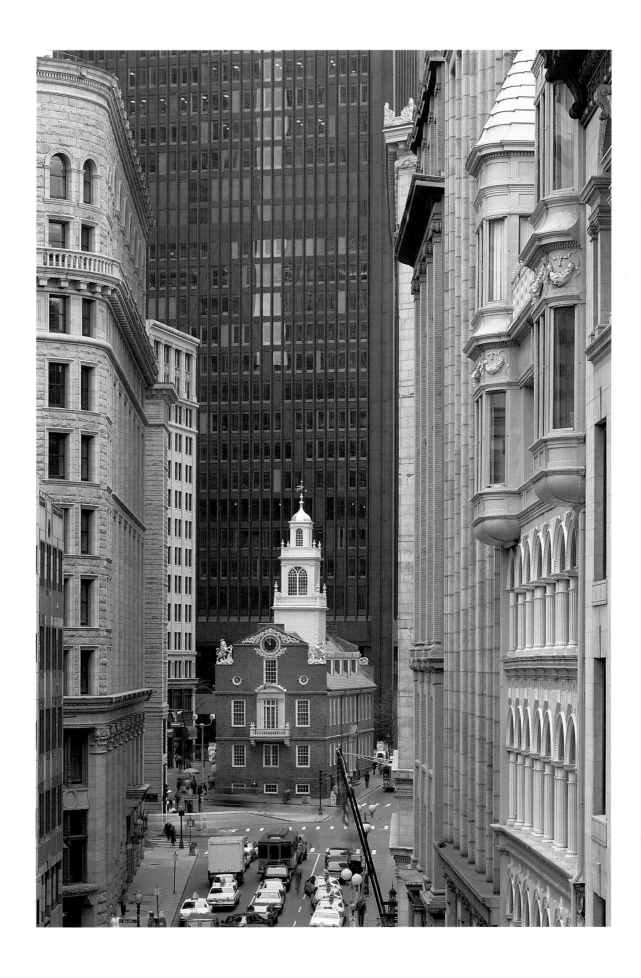

Mother Church, Christian Science Center   Old State House, State Street

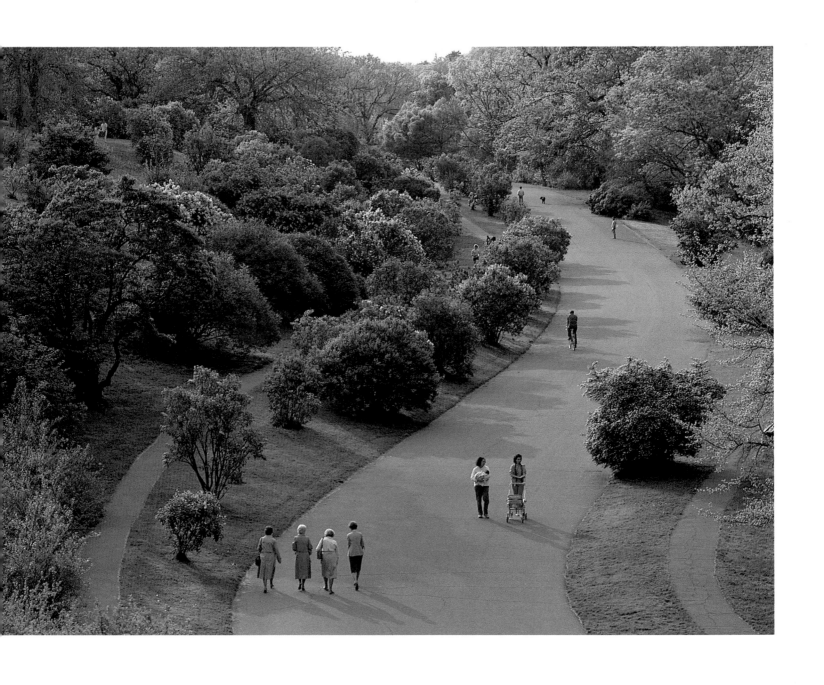

Lilacs on Bussey Hill, Arnold Arboretum

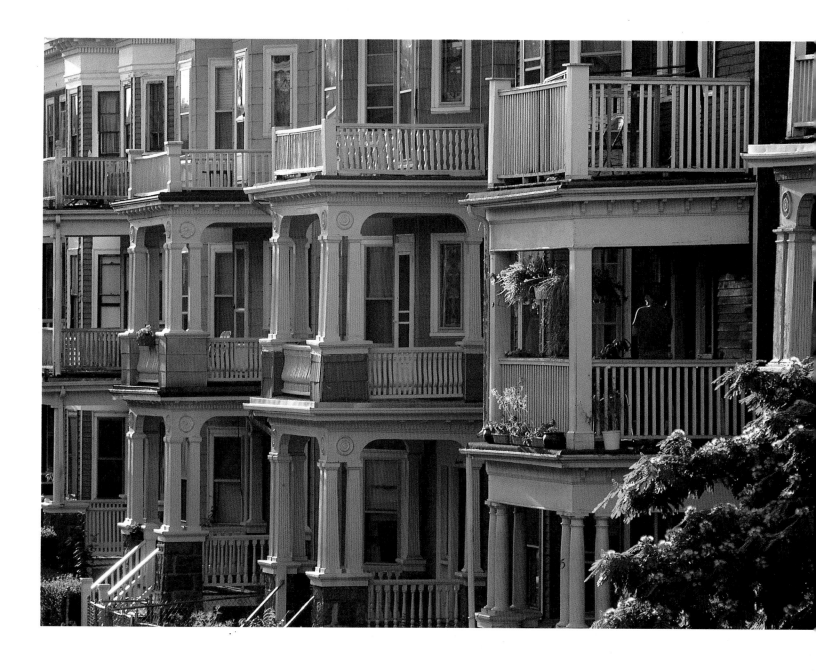

Three-decker houses, Dorchester   *Overleaf:* Financial District, from Harbor Towers

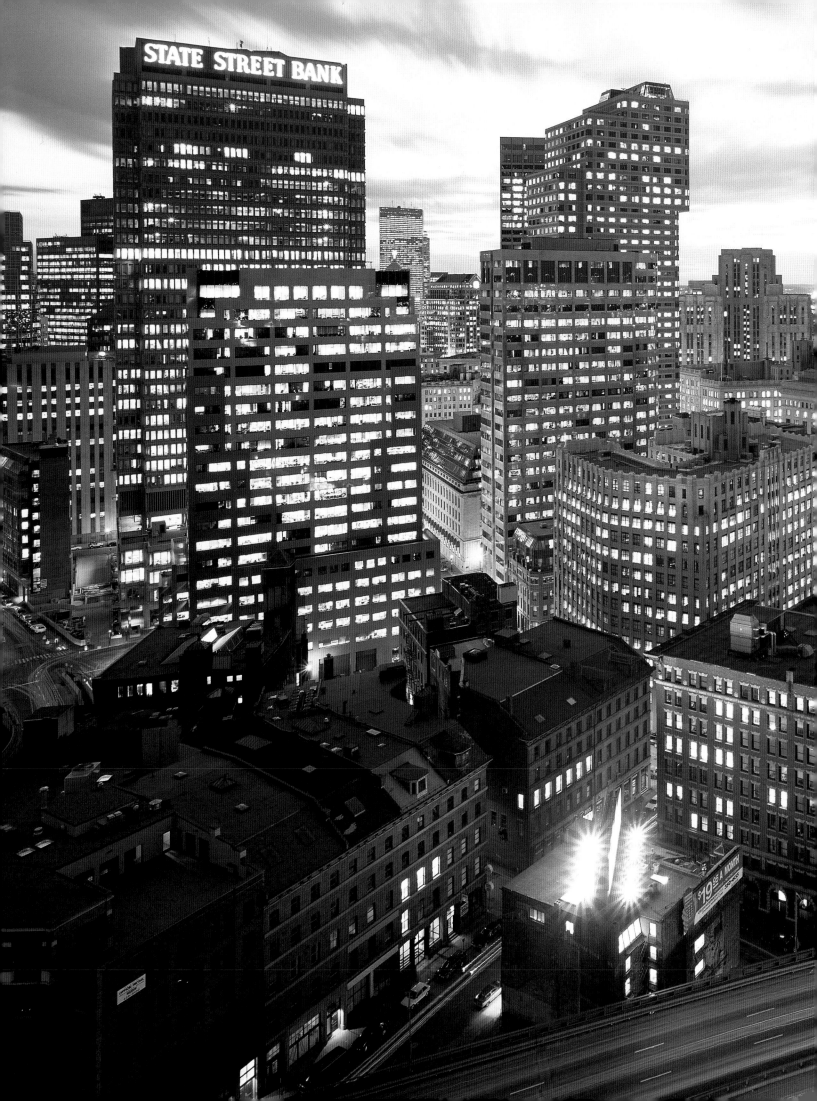

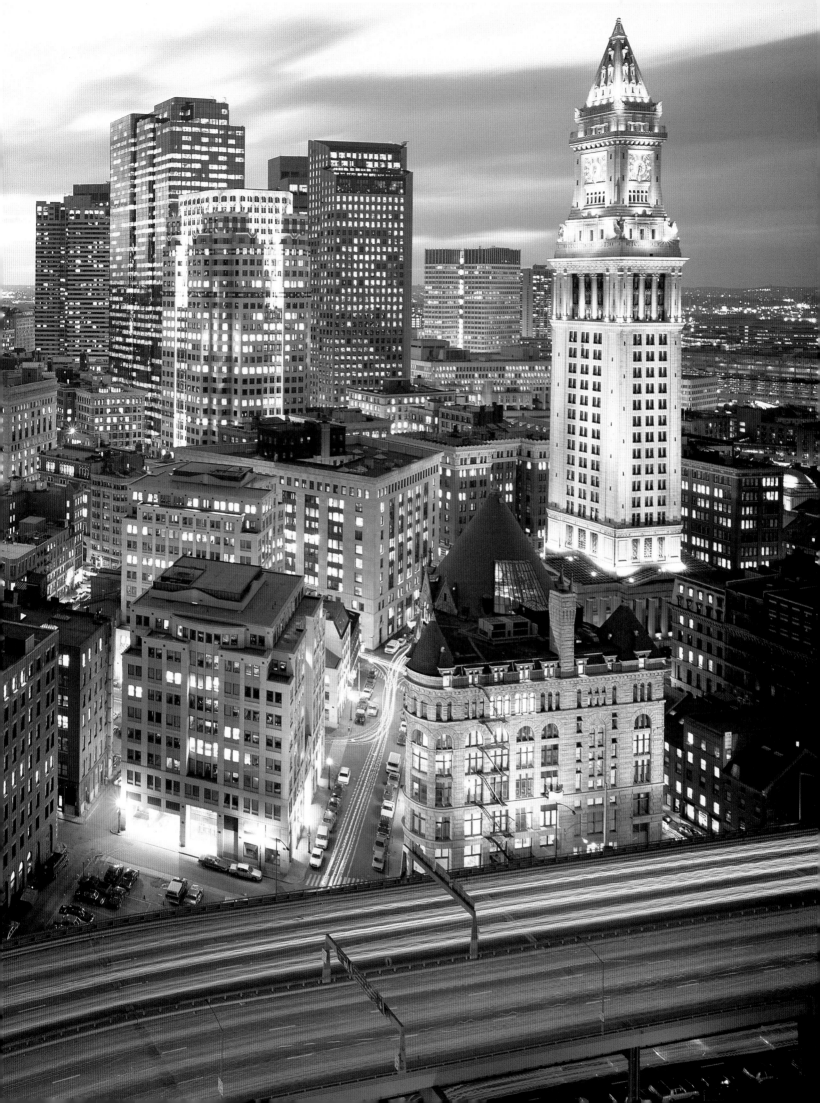

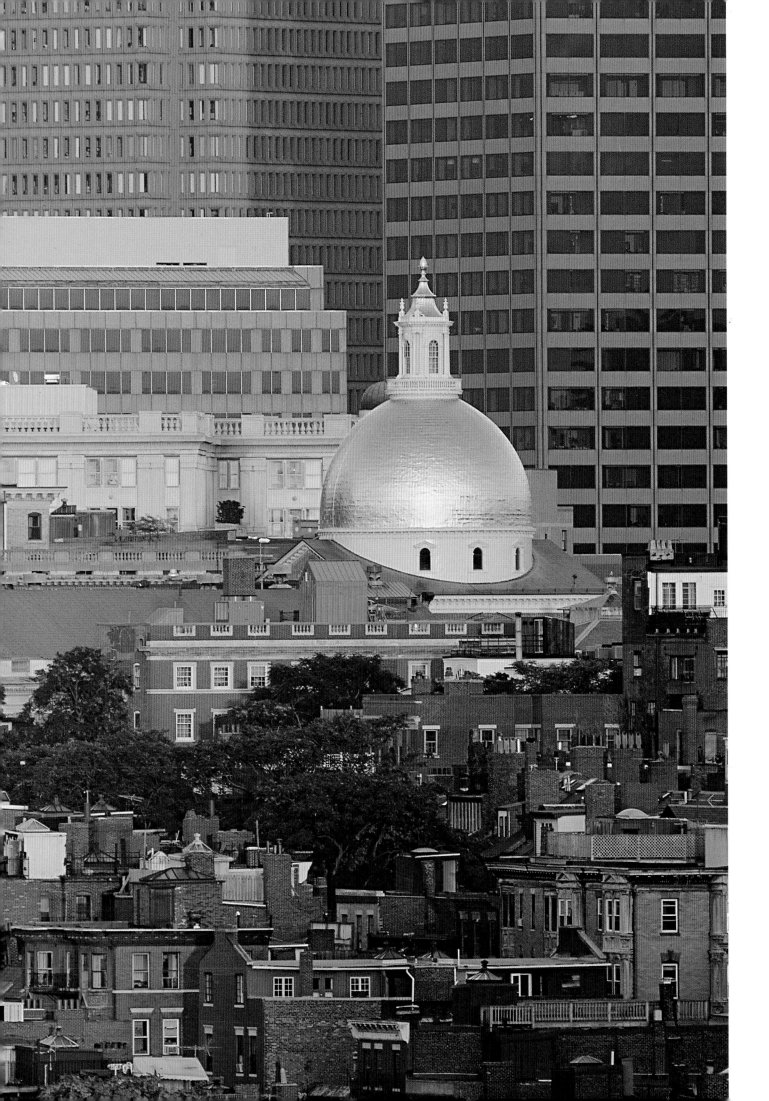

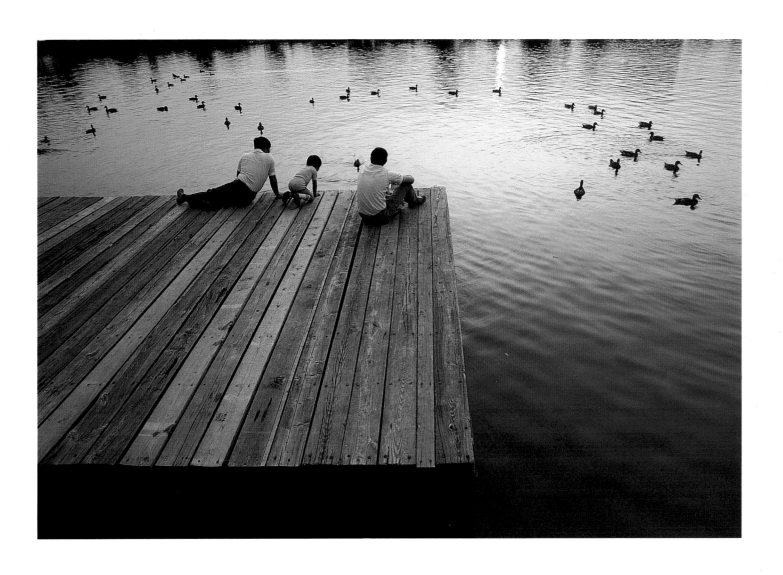

Evening with ducks, Charles River Esplanade

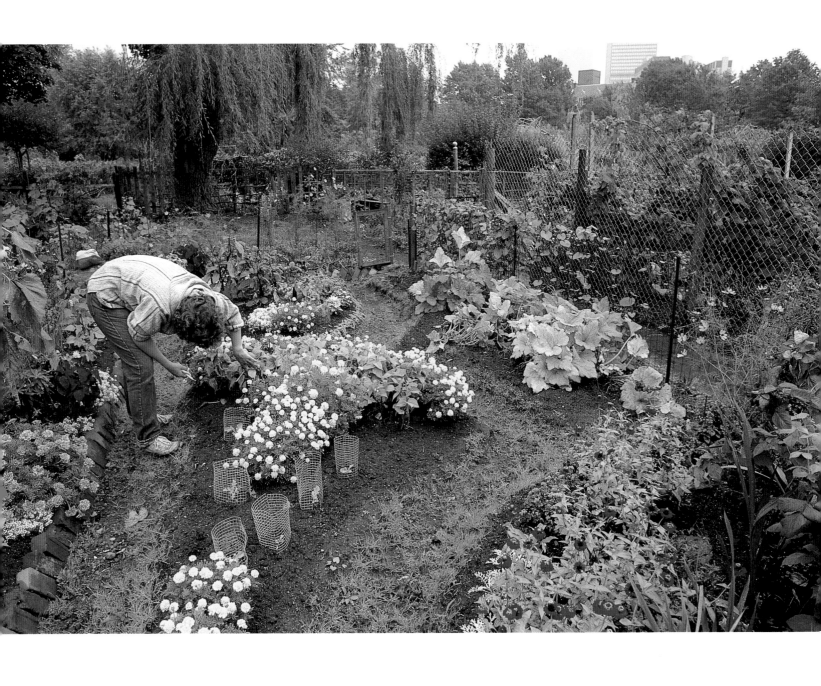

Family garden, the Fenway

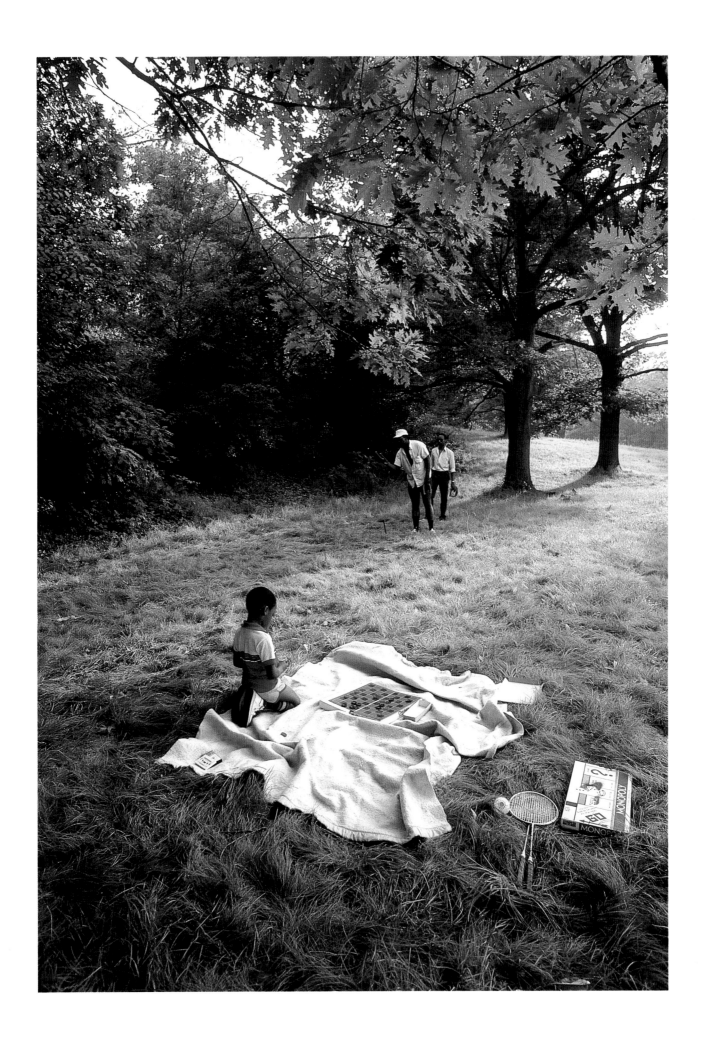

Summer picnic, Franklin Park   *Overleaf:* The Isabella Stewart Gardner Museum courtyard

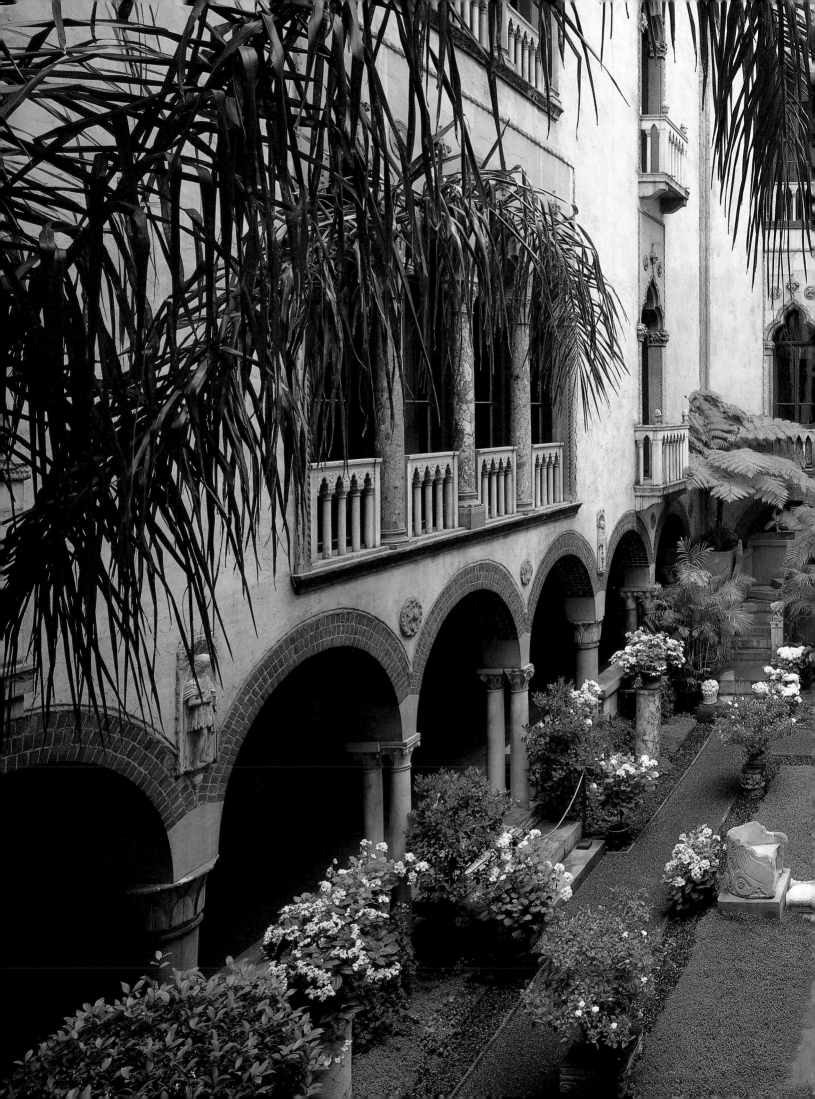

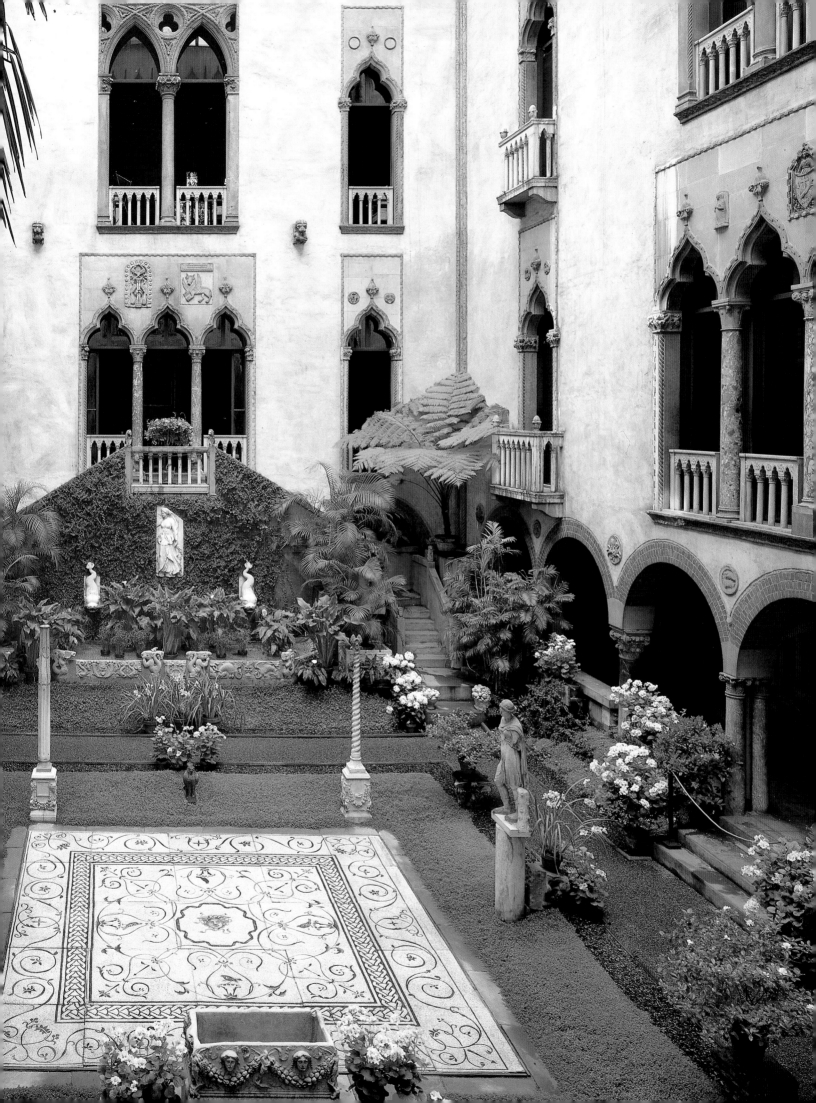

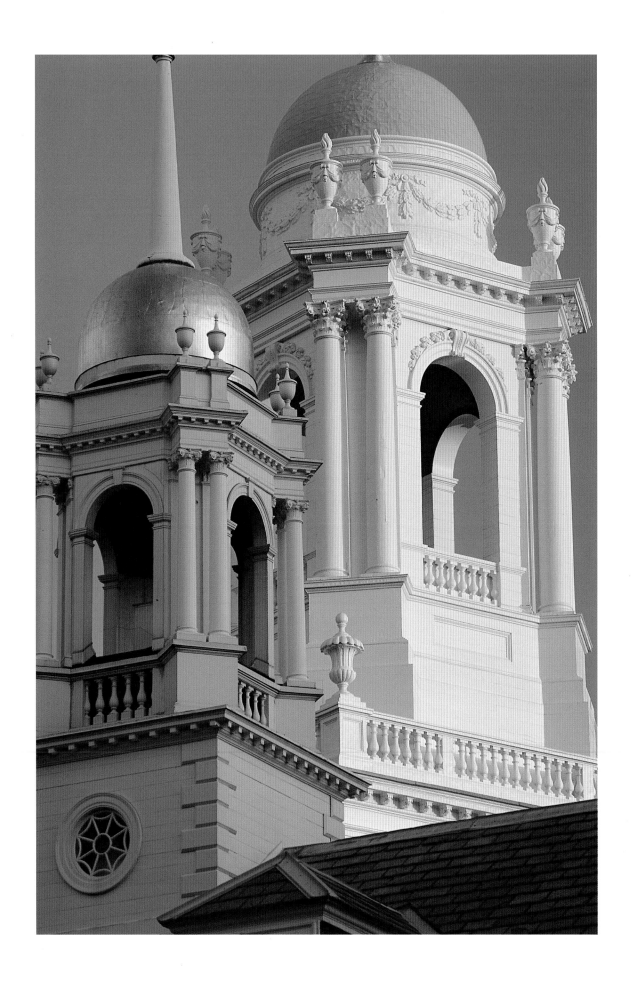

Winthrop and Eliot house towers, Harvard

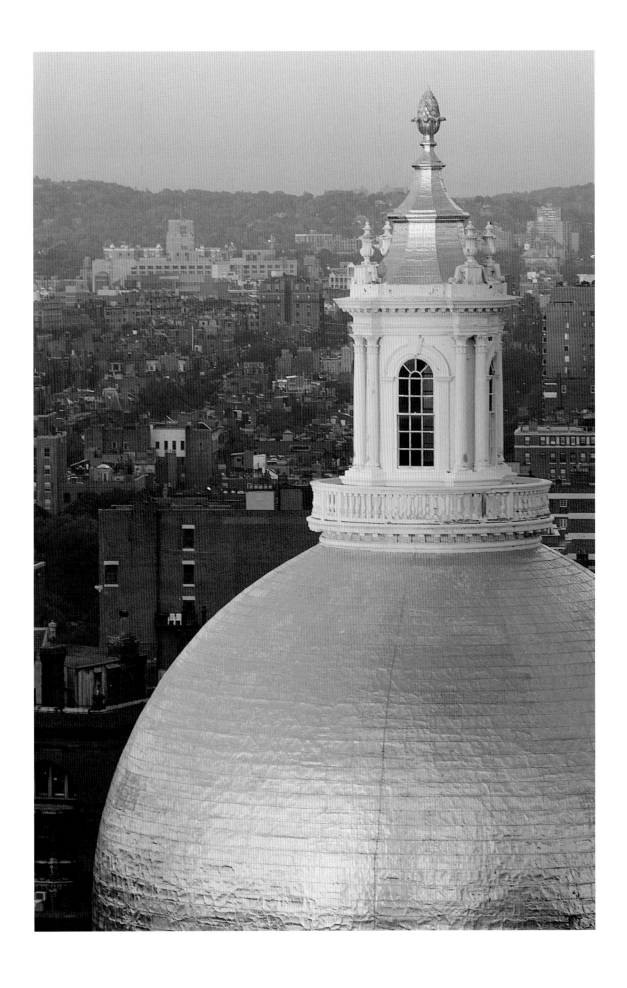

Gilded Bulfinch dome, State House

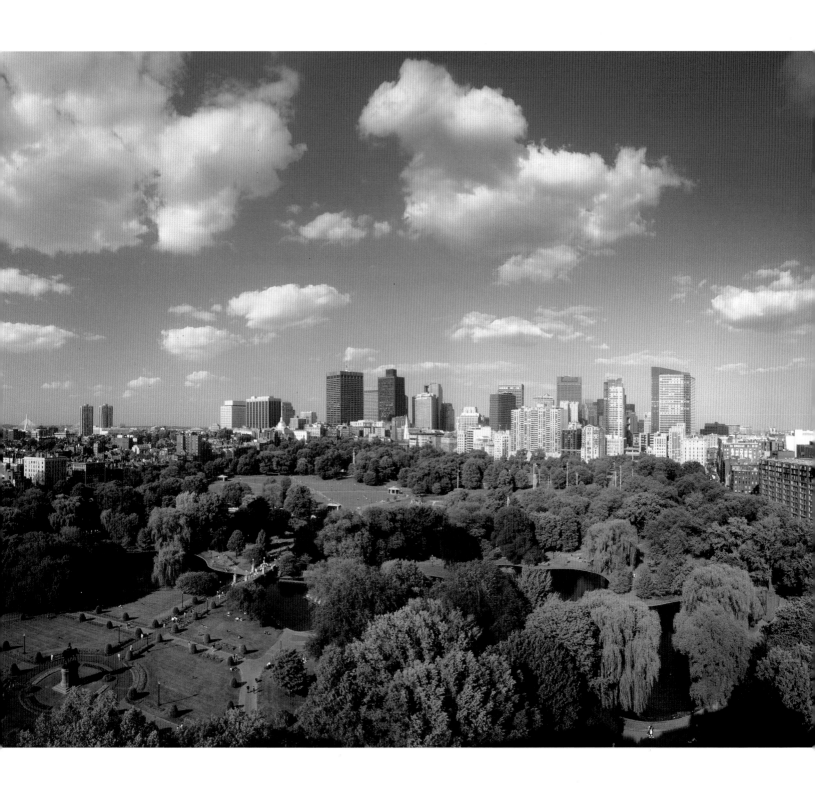

Public Garden and Boston Common

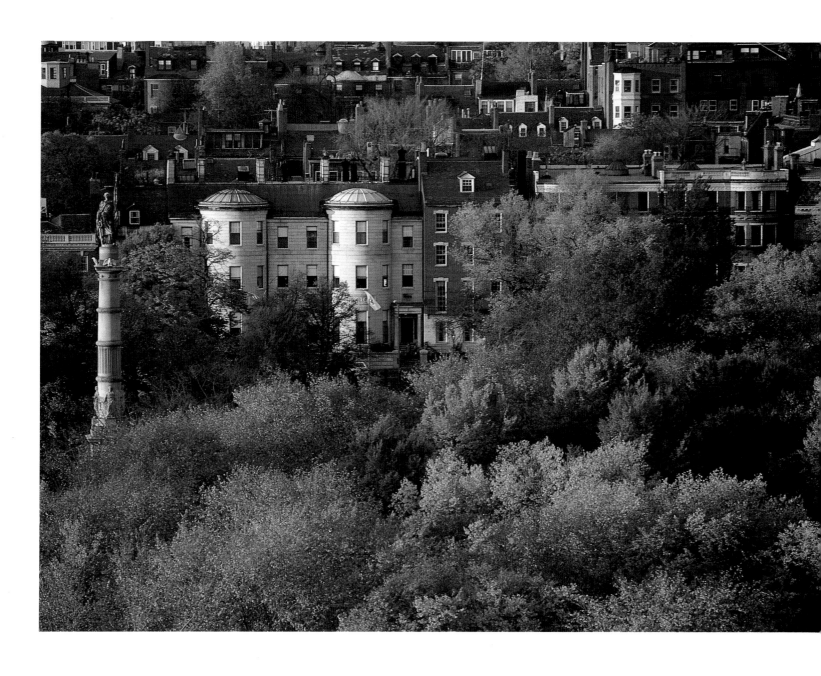

Beacon Street, Boston Common autumn   *Overleaf:* Back Bay skyline and Longfellow Bridge

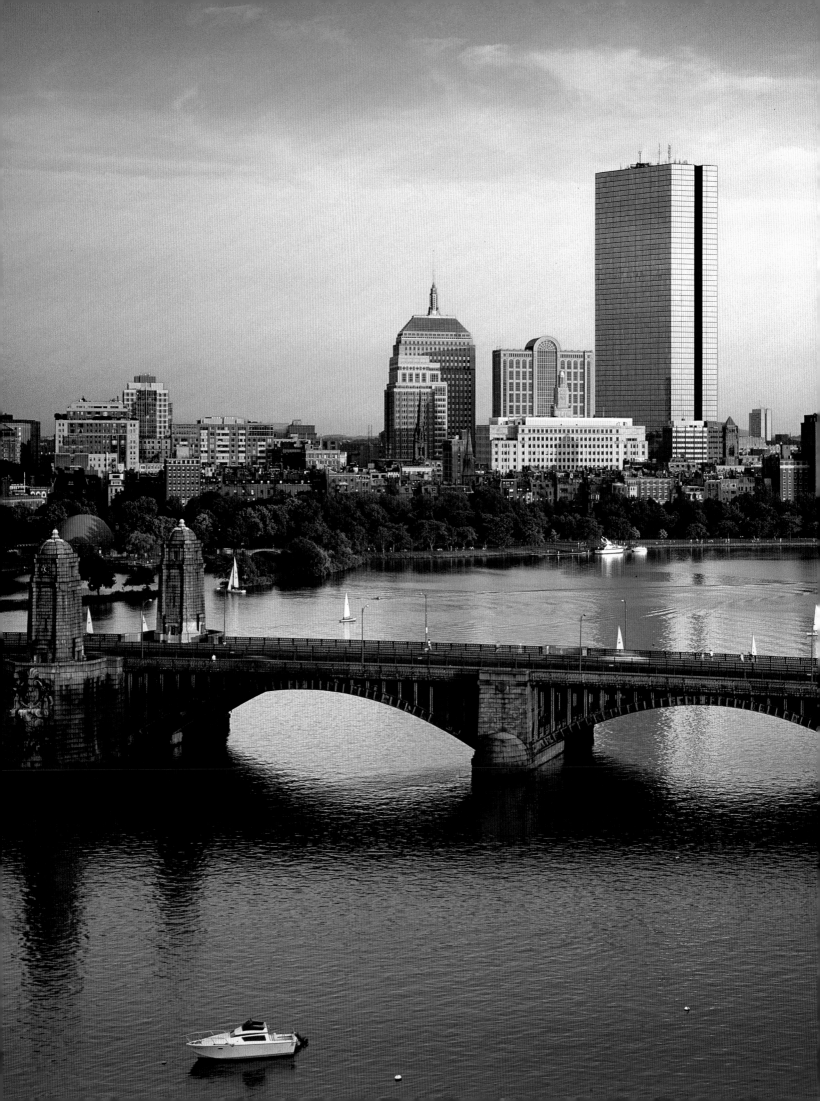

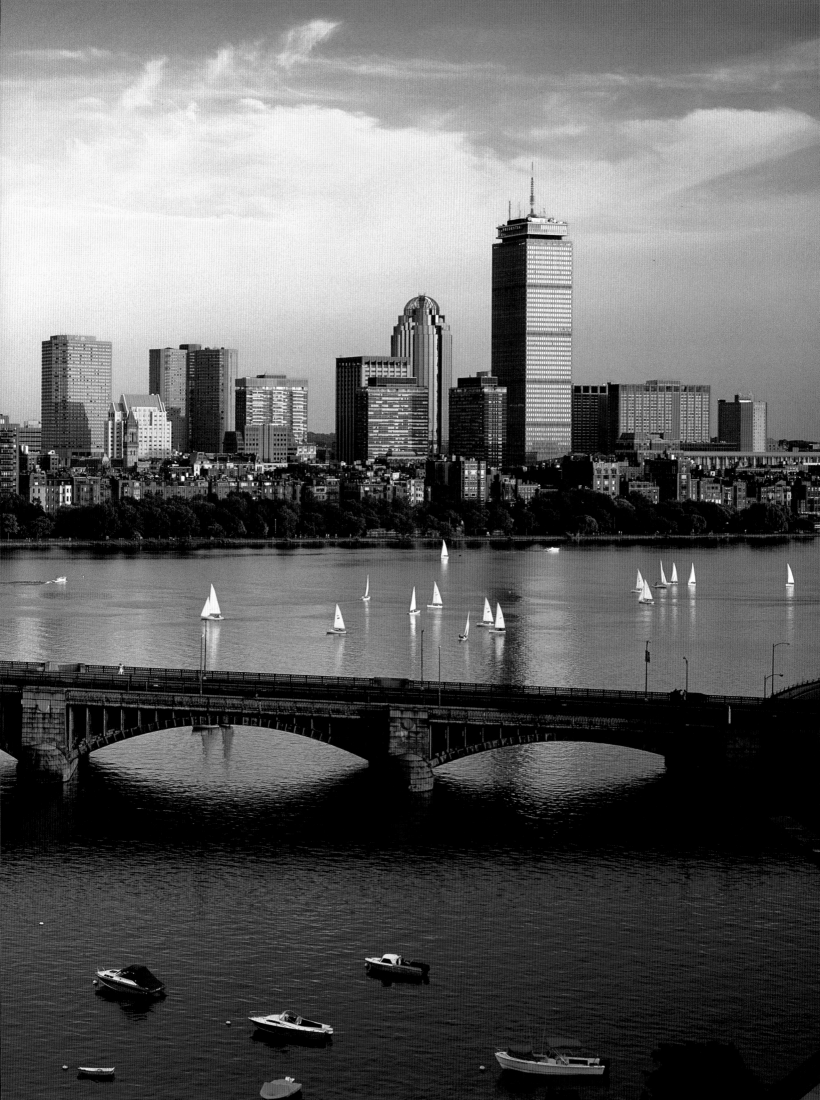

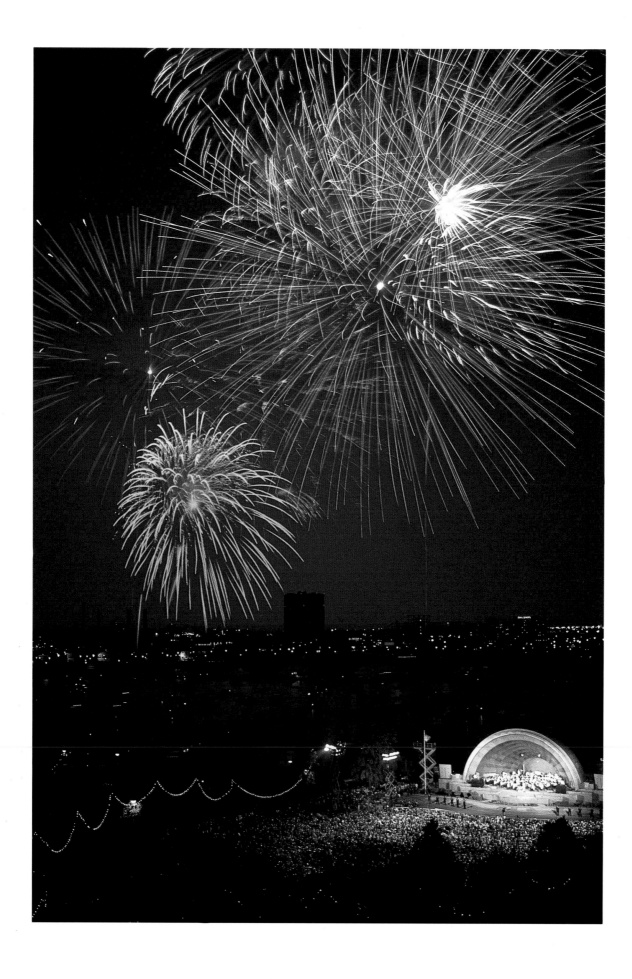

July Fourth fireworks, Boston Pops at Hatch Shell

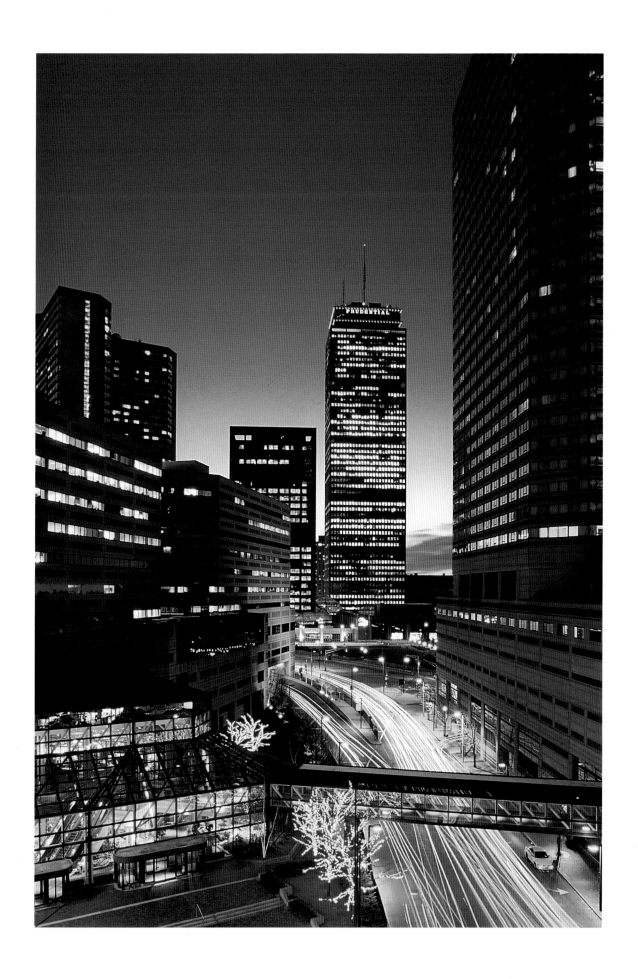

Copley Place

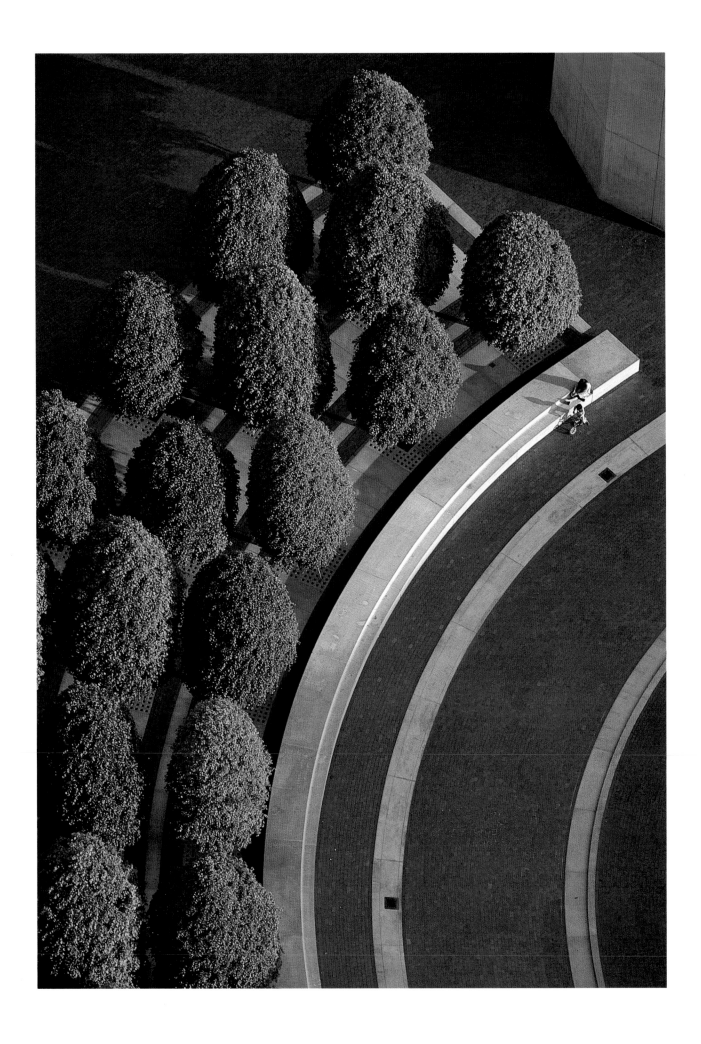

Spring afternoon, Christian Science Center

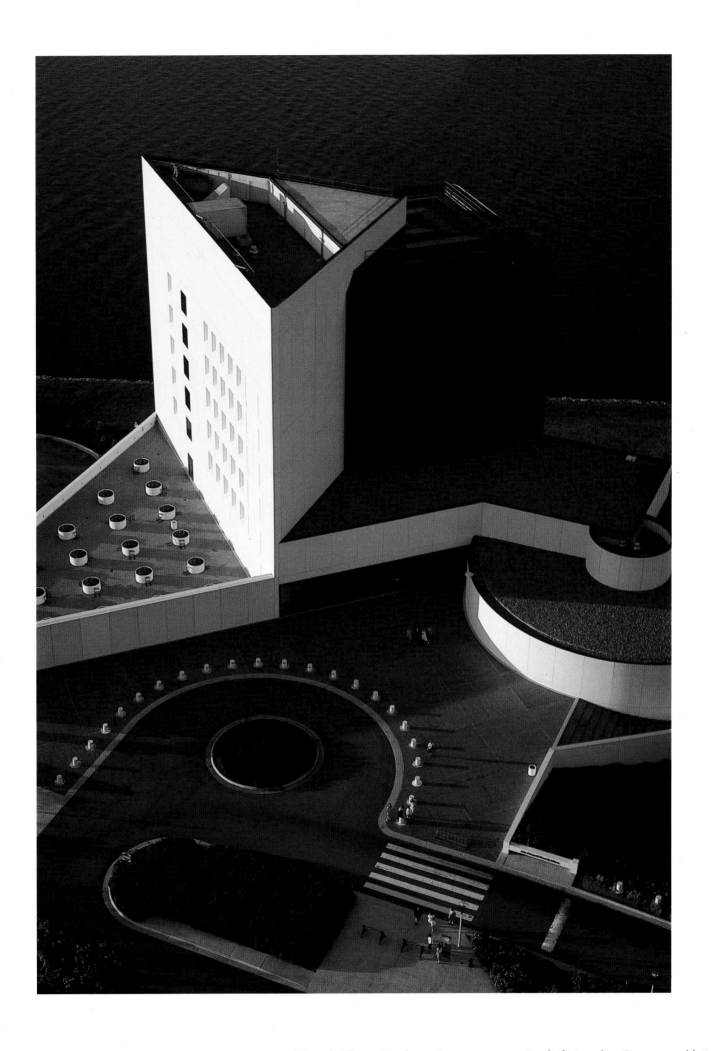

Kennedy Library, Dorchester Bay   *Overleaf:* Magnolias, Commonwealth Avenue

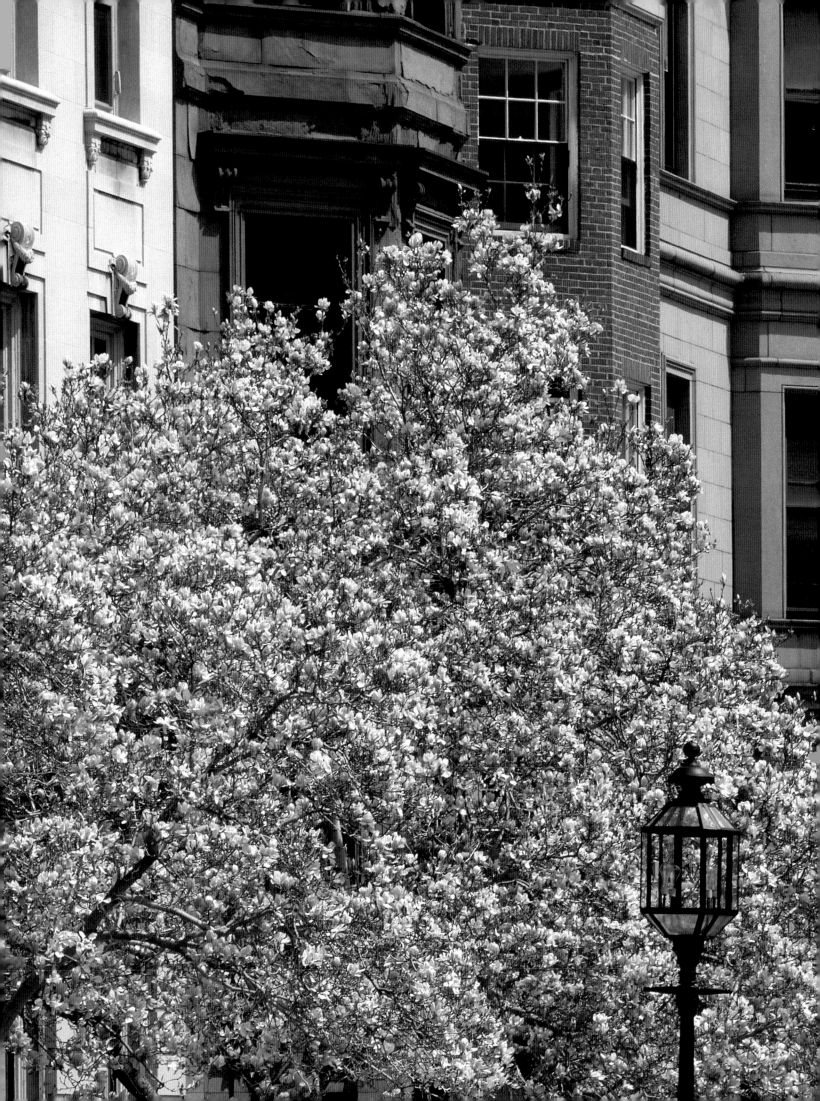

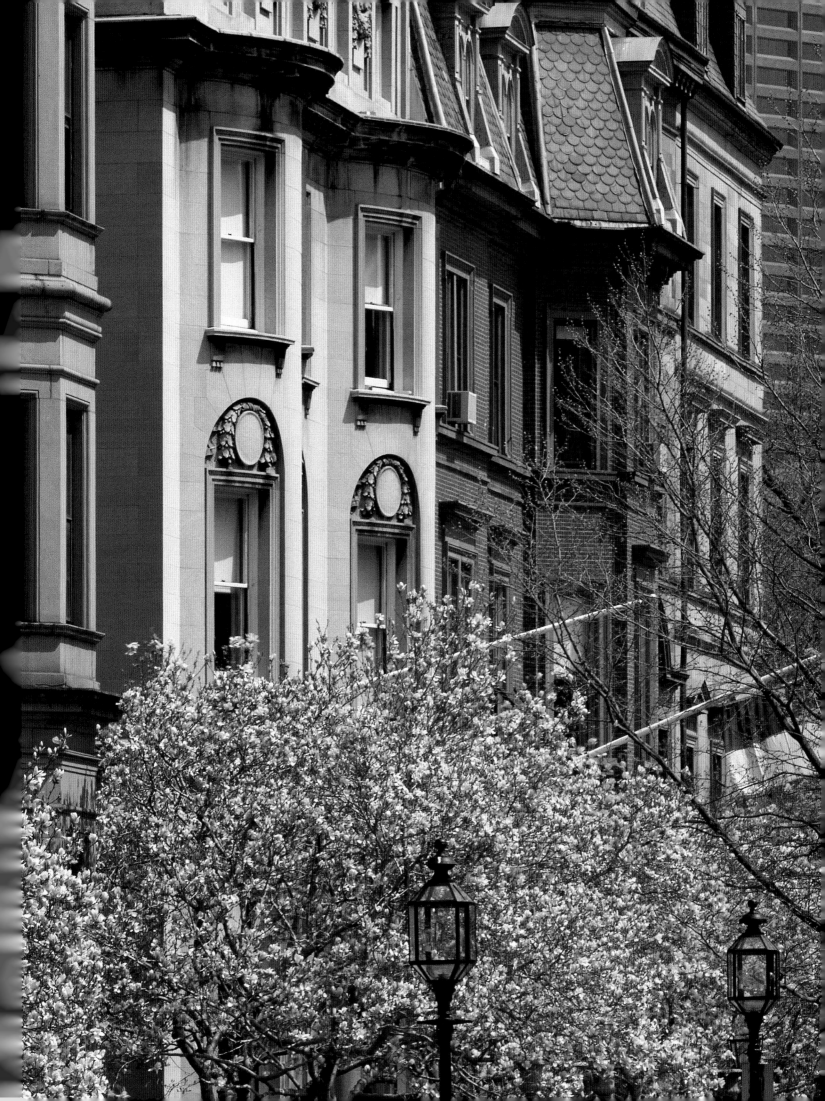

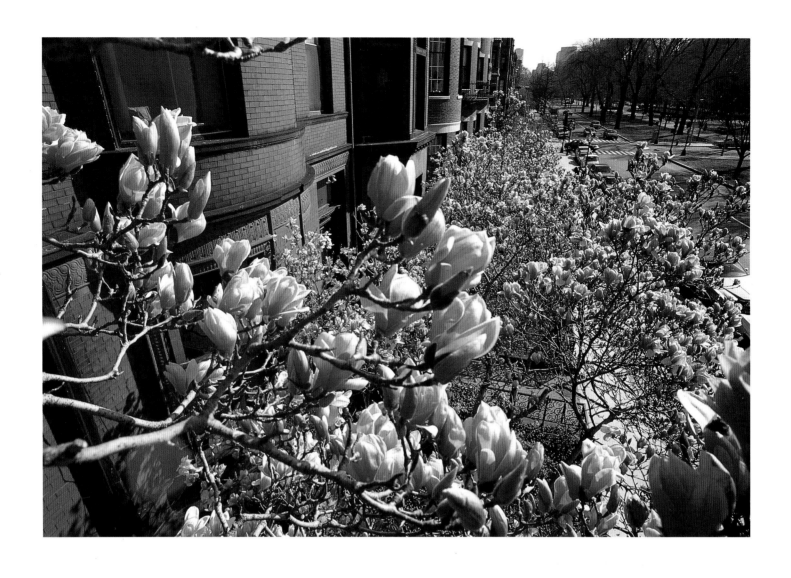

Magnolia blossoms, Commonwealth Avenue   Mount Vernon Street, Beacon Hill

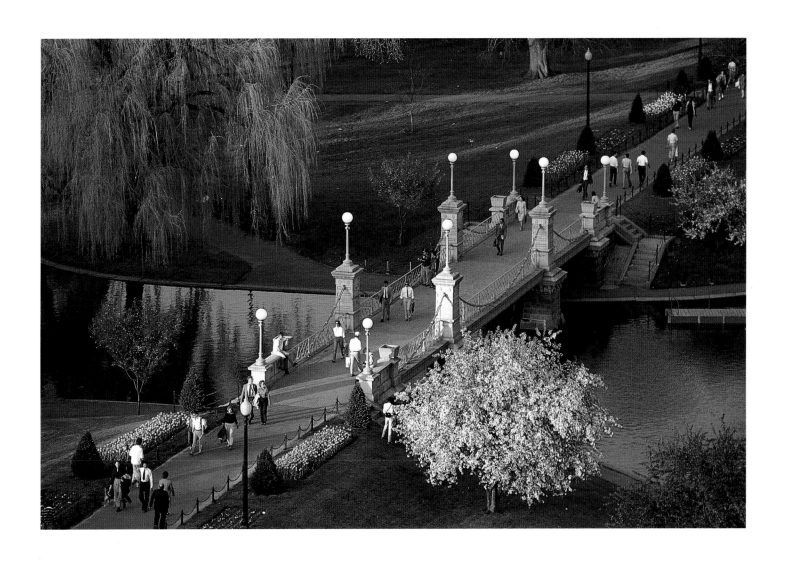

Springtime crossing, the Public Garden

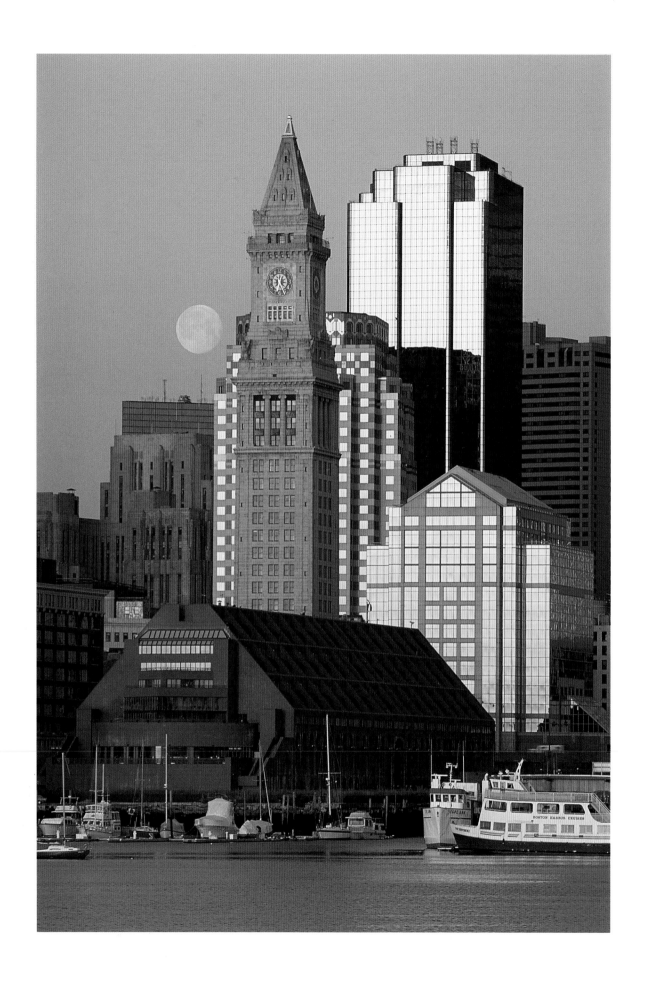

Harbor at sunrise, full moon

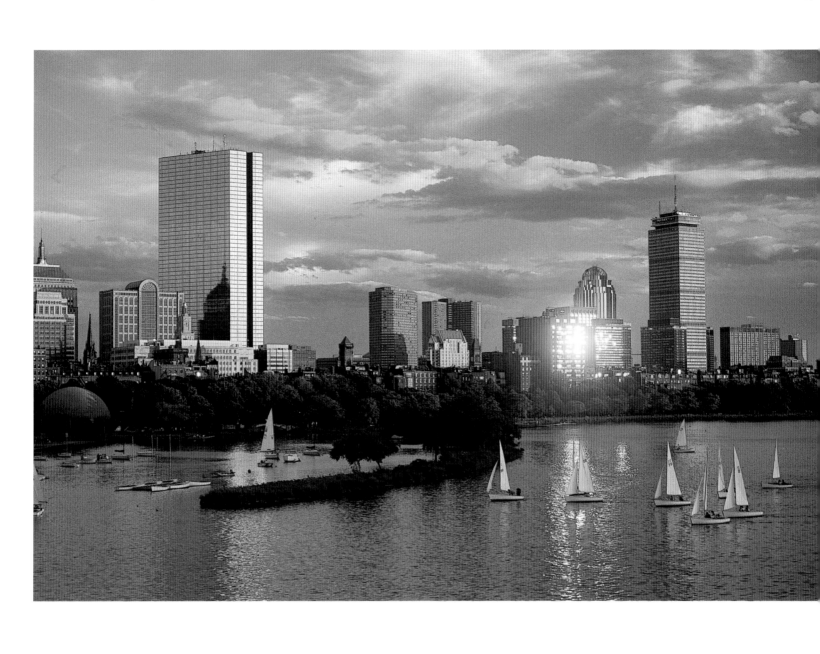

Back Bay, Charles River

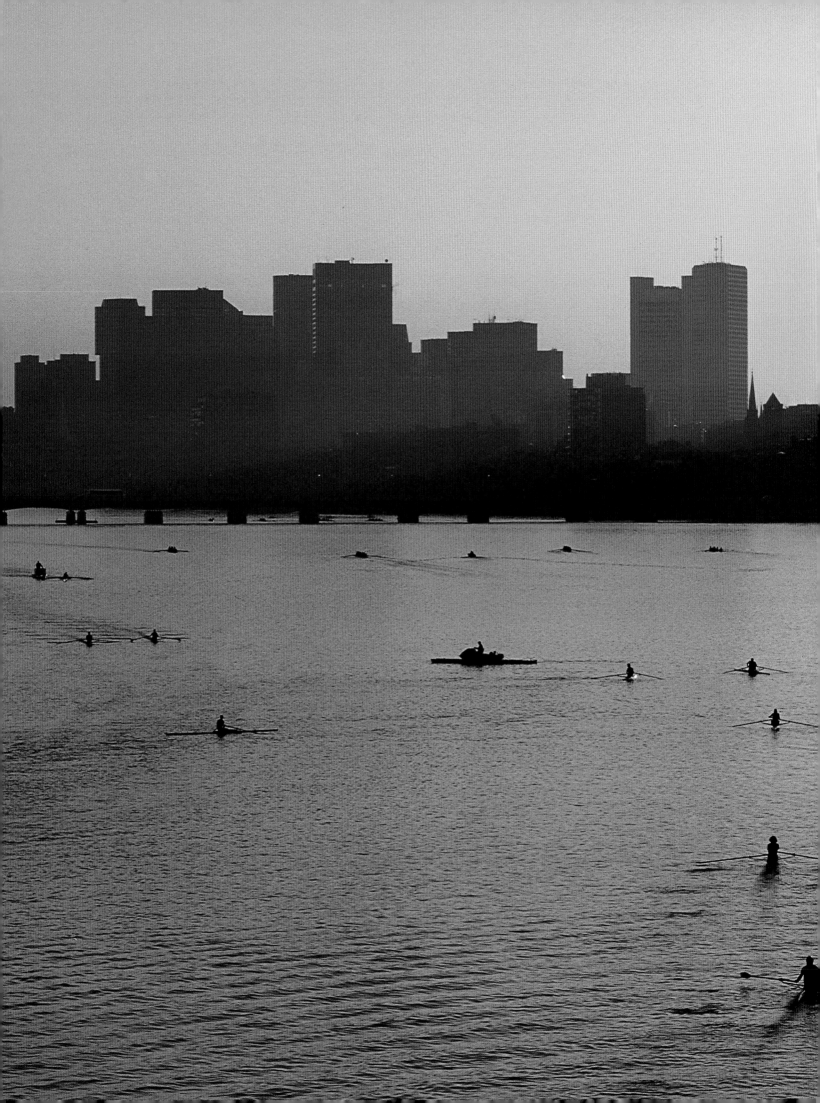

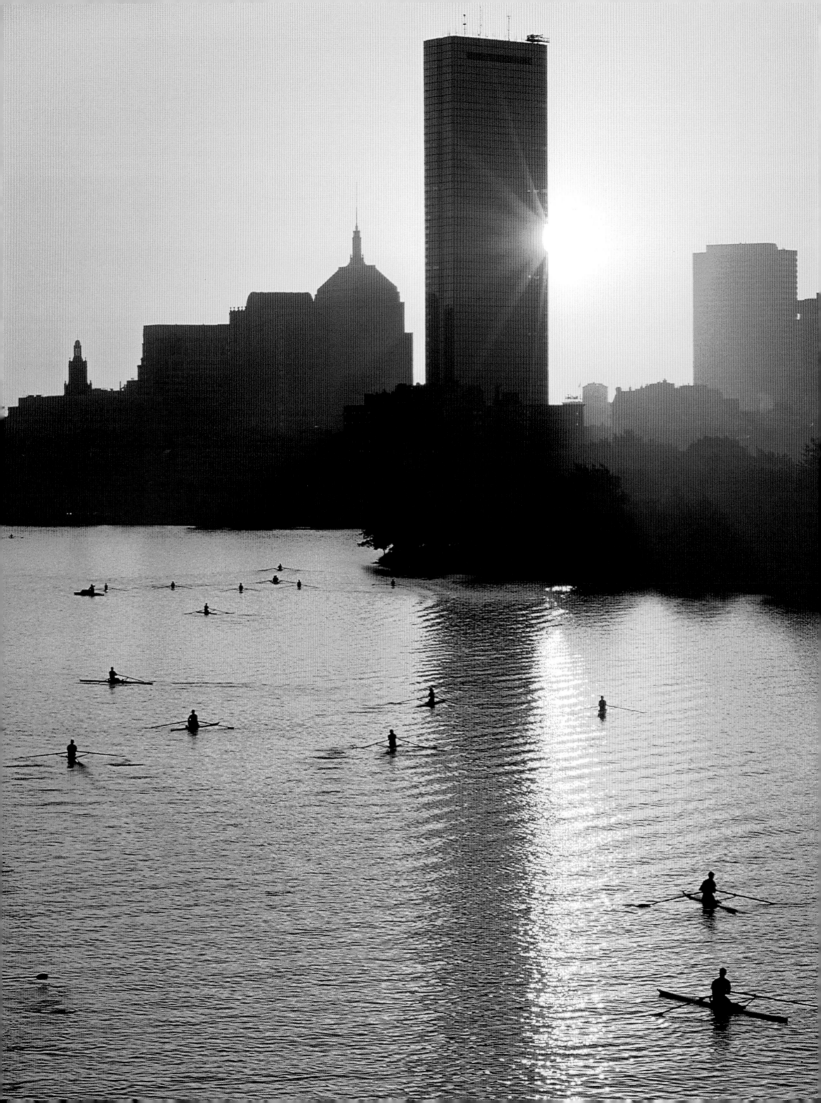

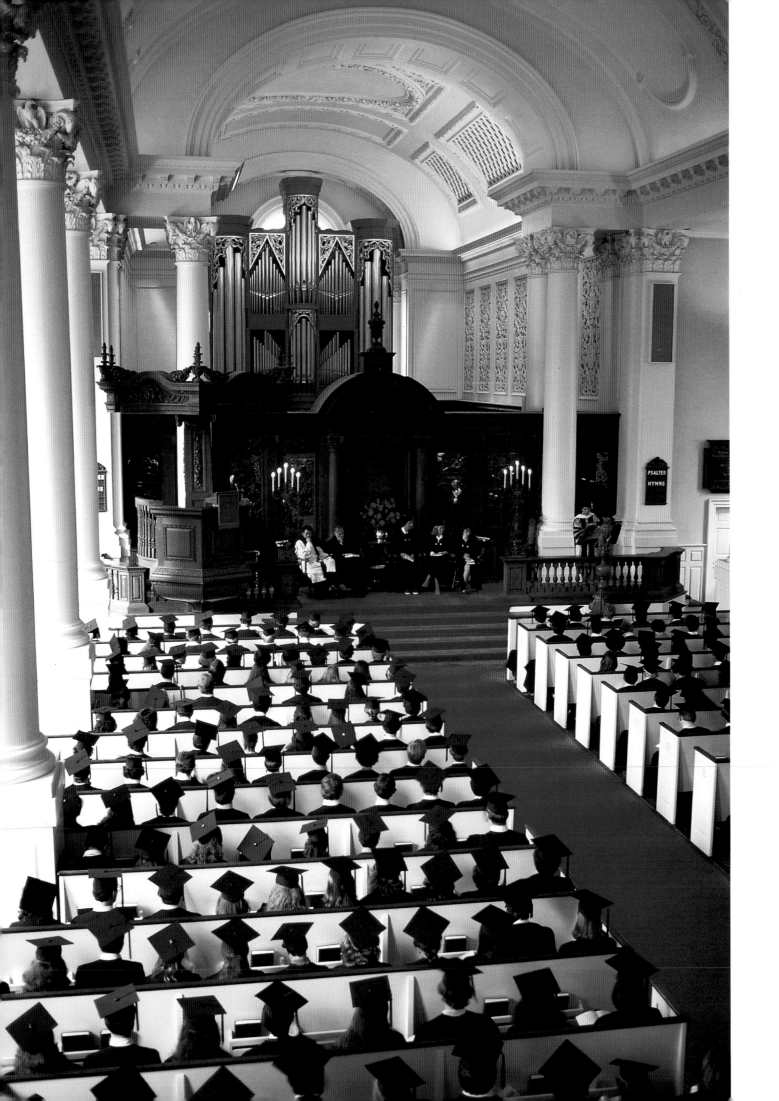

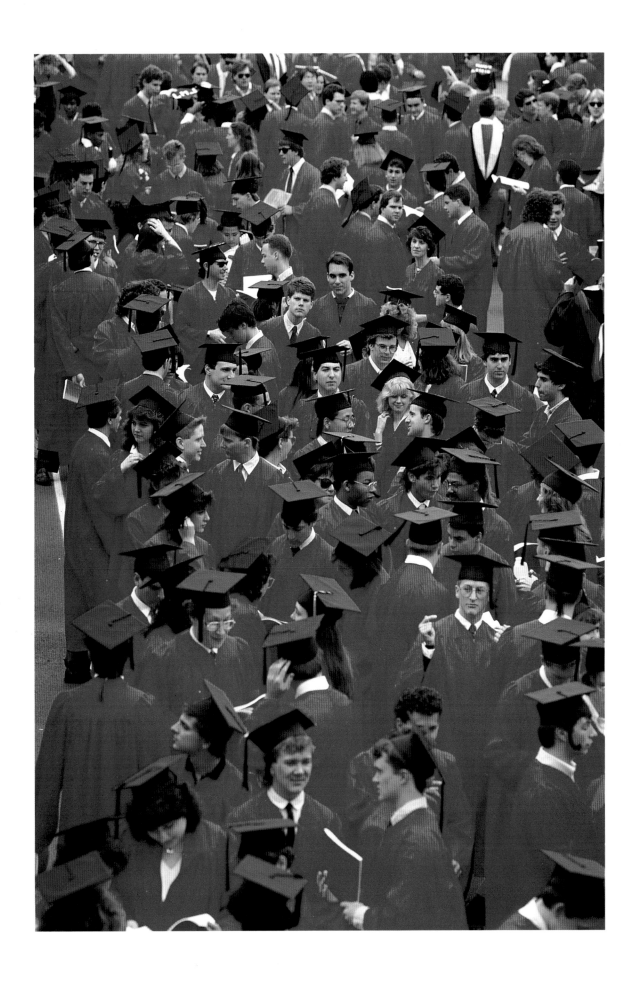

Harvard graduation, Memorial Church
BU graduates, Nickerson Field

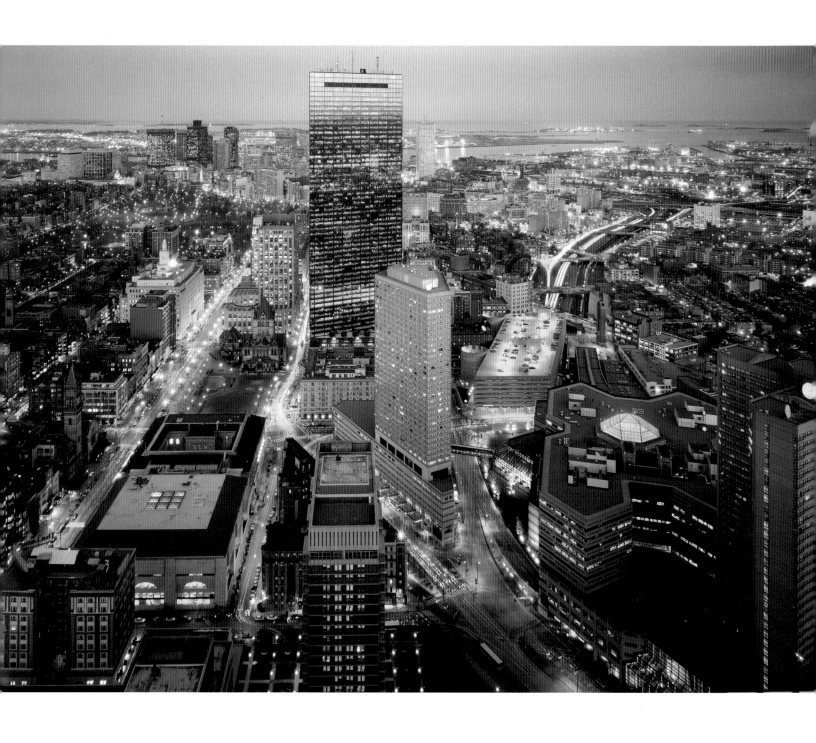

Back Bay to South Boston, winter moonlight

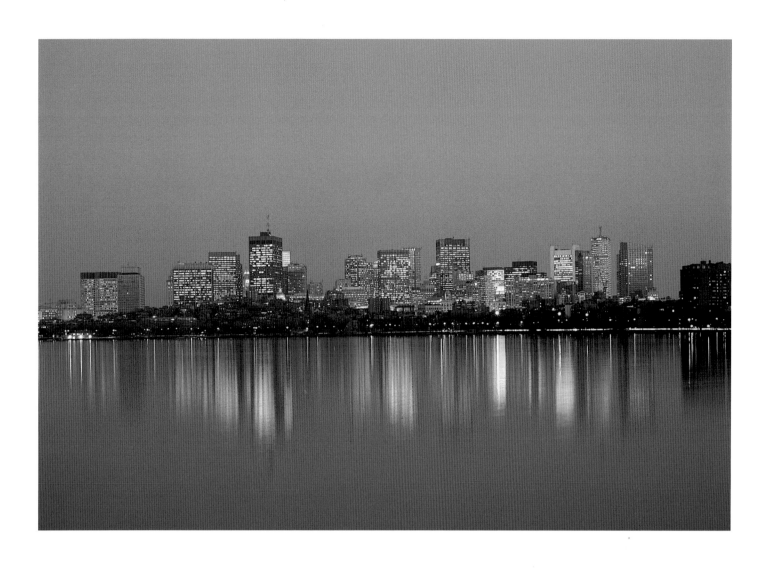

Beacon Hill, Charles River   *Overleaf:* Museum of Fine Arts

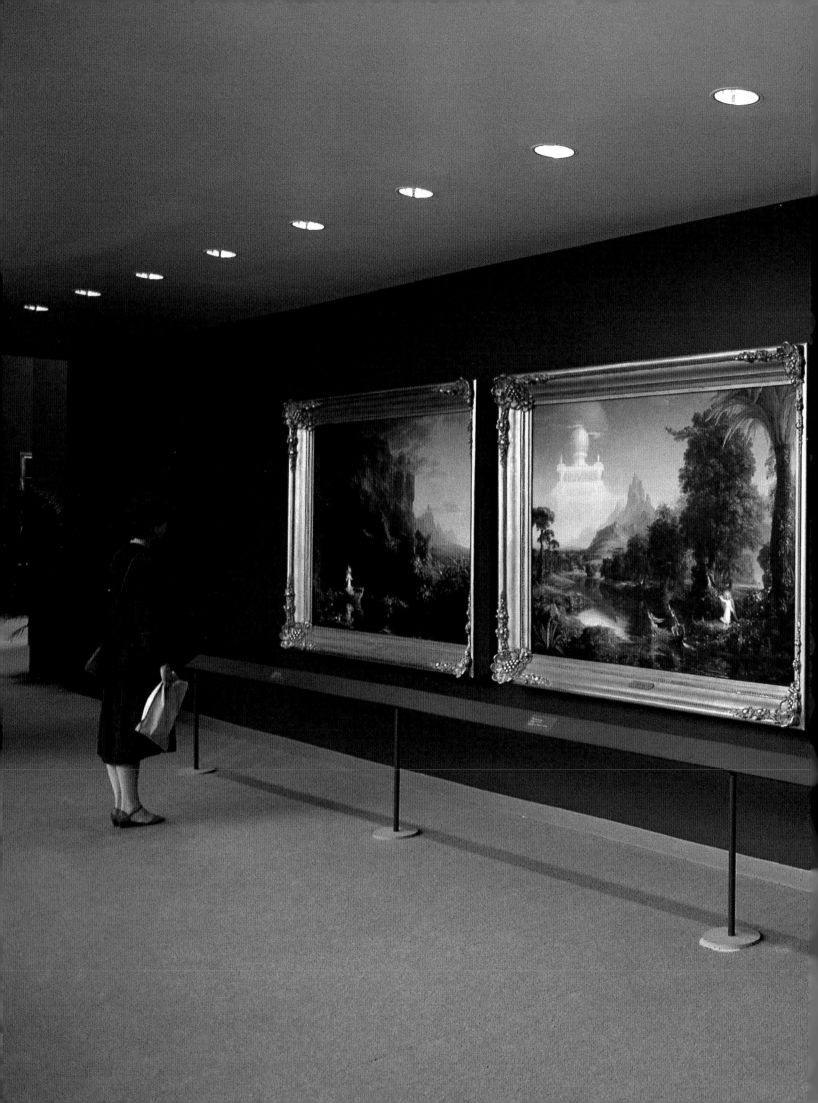

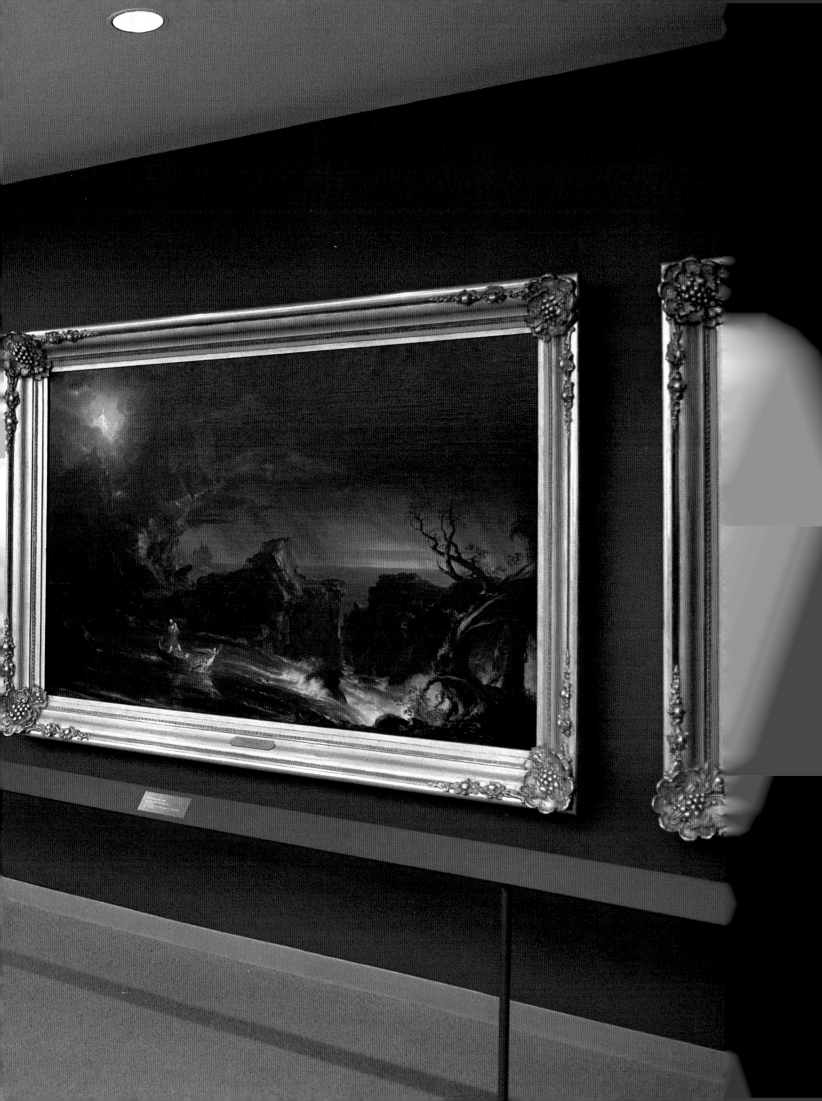

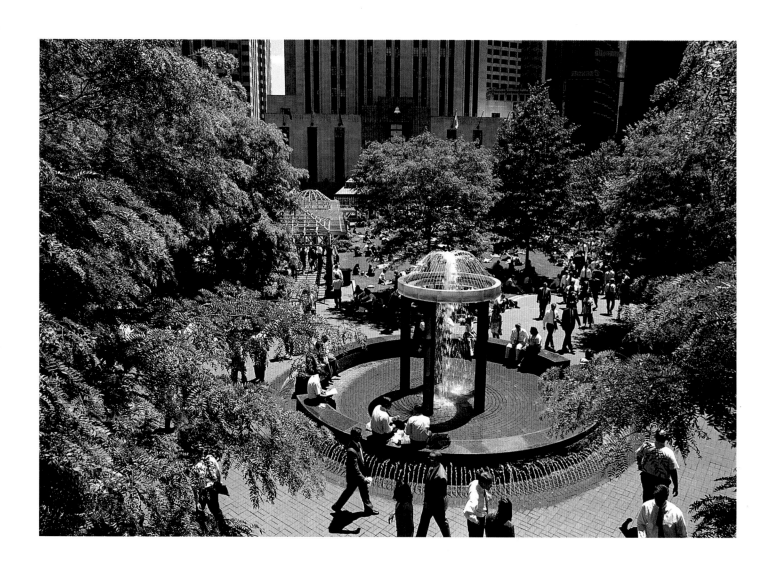

Post Office Square

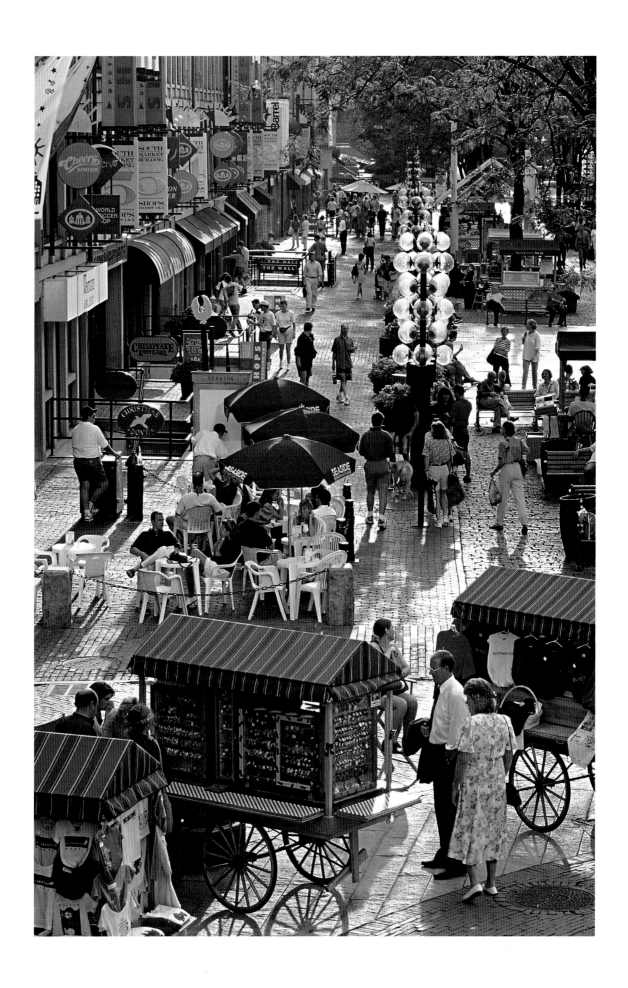

Quincy Market

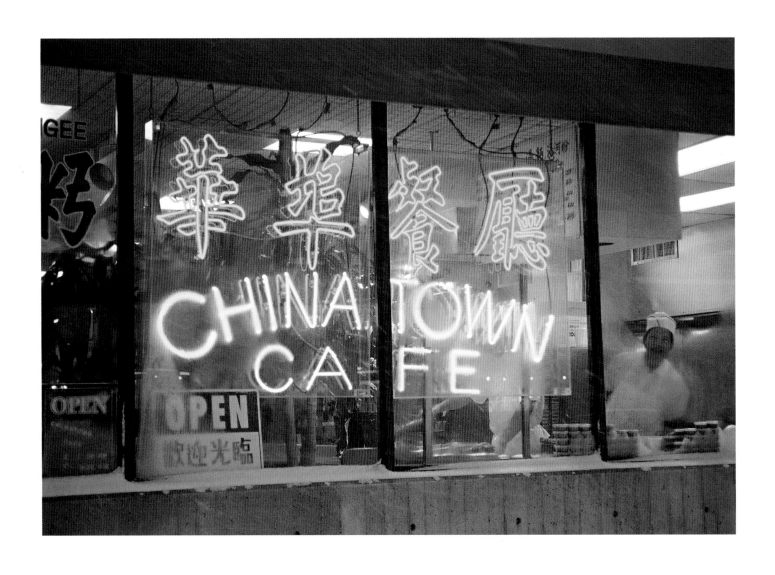

Harrison Avenue, Tai Tung village

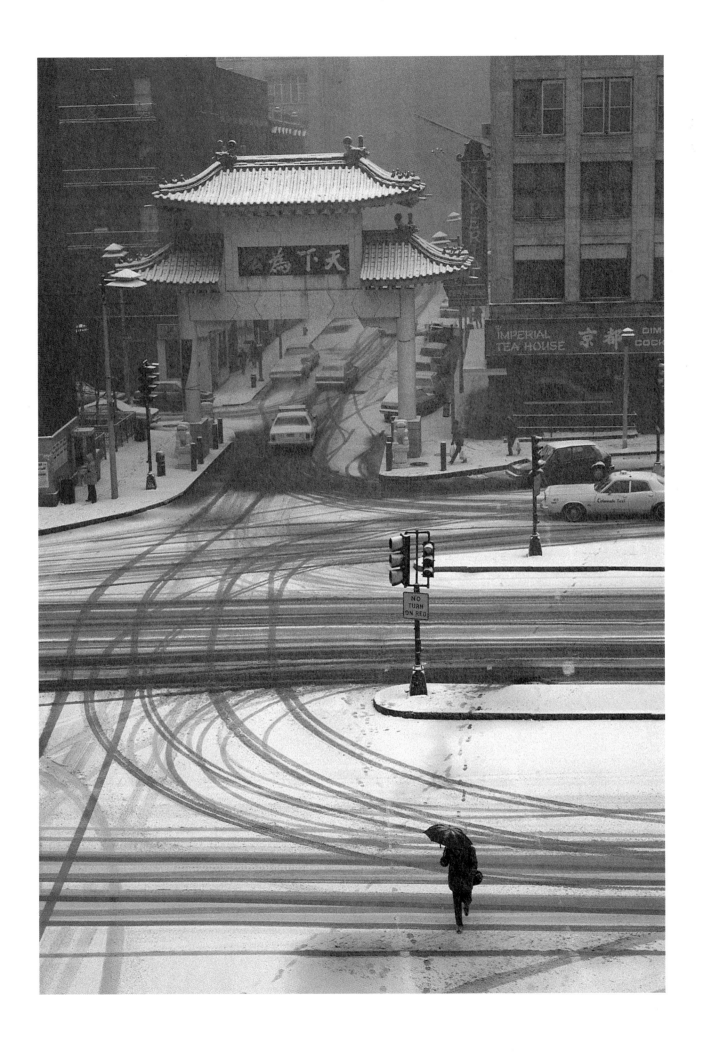

Beach Street entrance, Chinatown

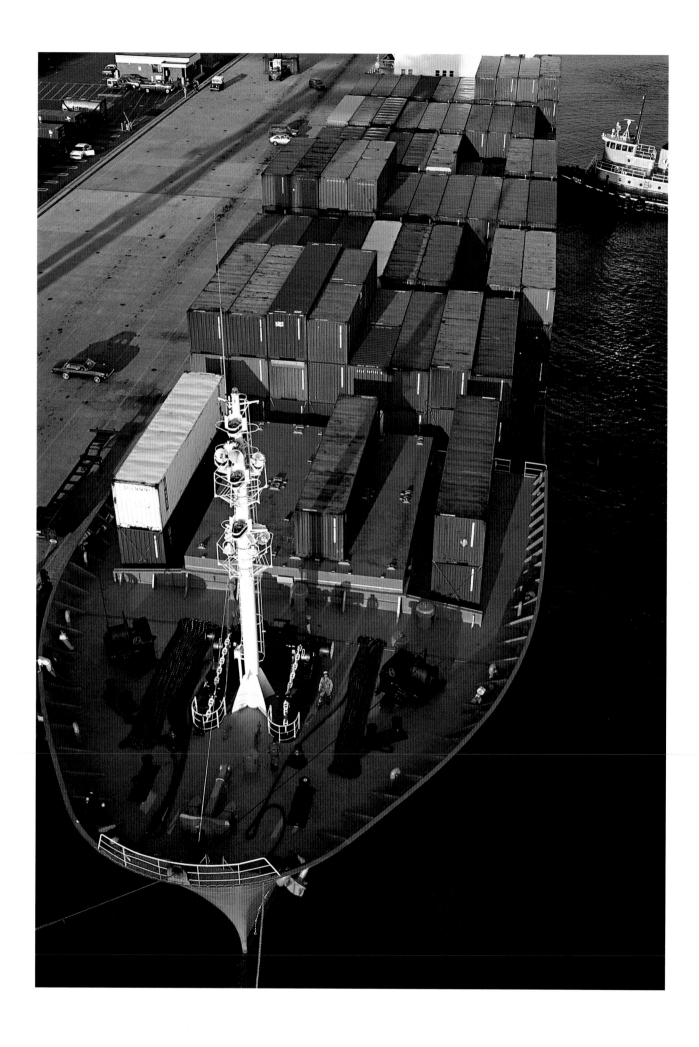

Container Cargo, South Boston

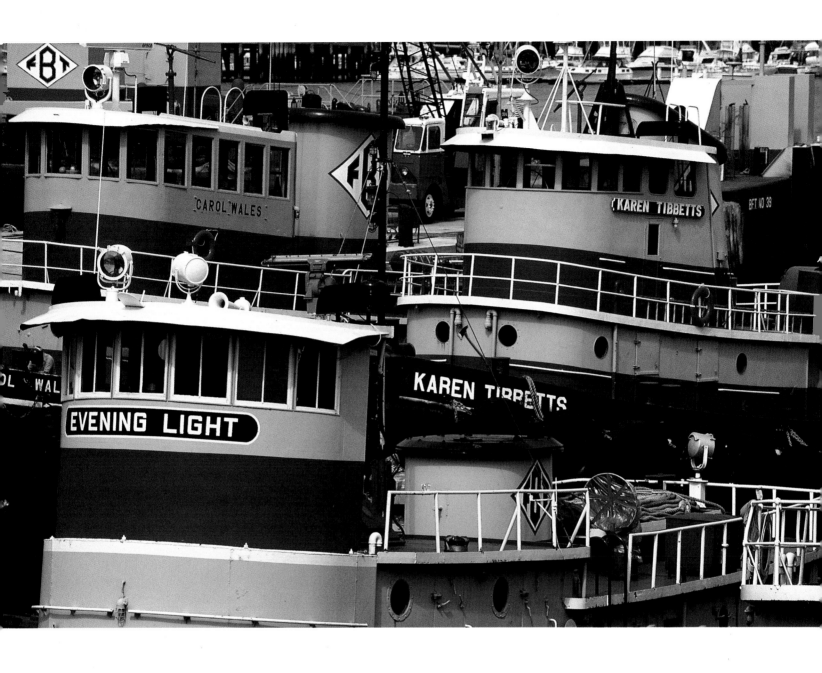

Tugboat piers, East Boston   *Overleaf:* "Holy Hornblowers," First Baptist Church, Commonwealth Avenue

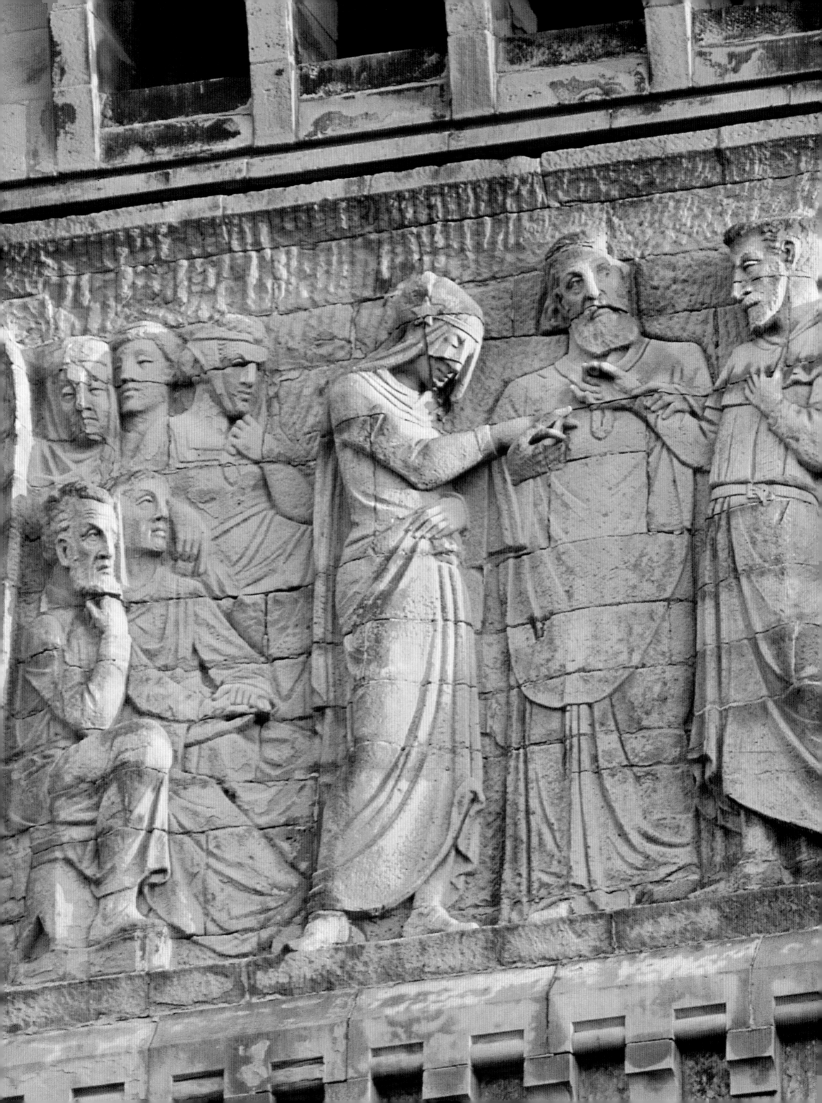

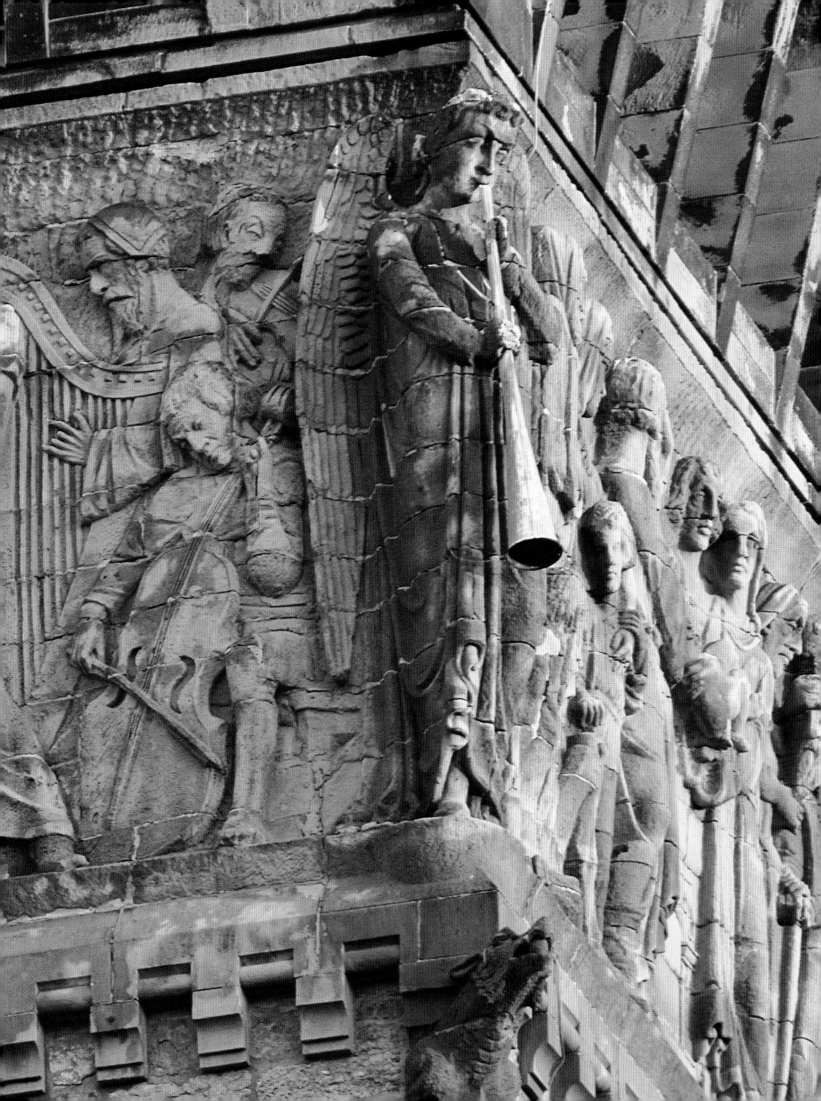

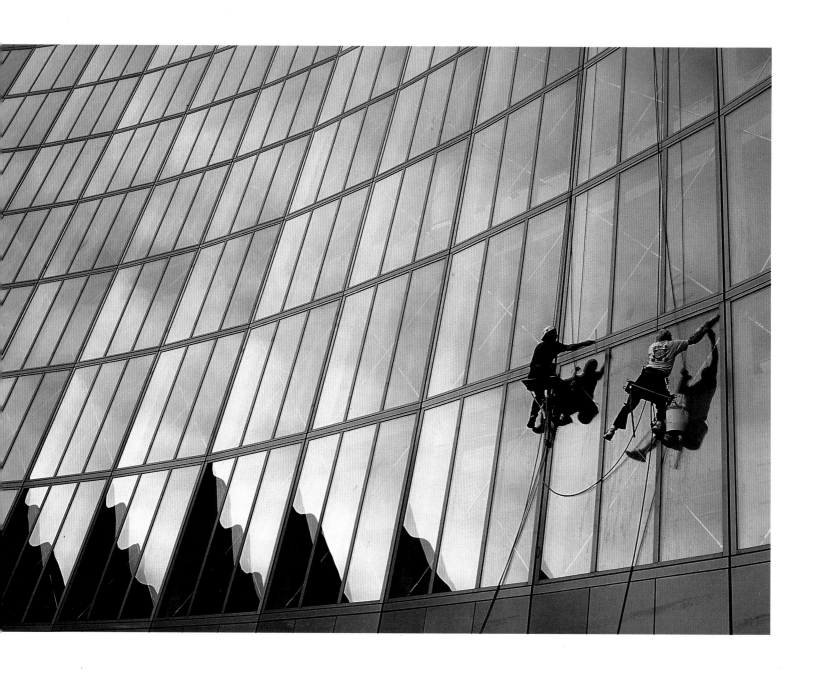

Fan pier windows

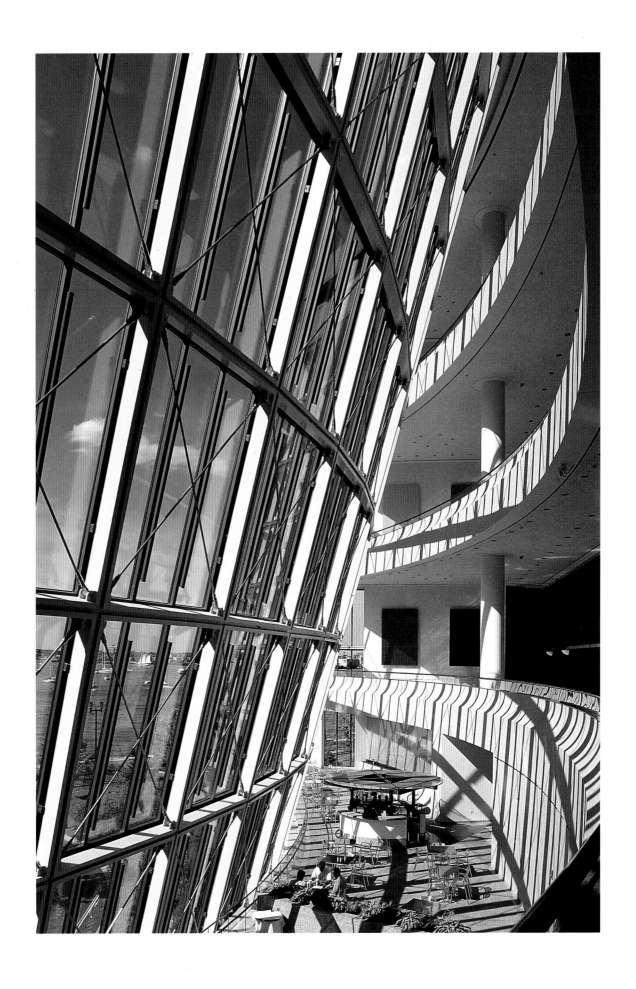

Federal Courthouse, summer afternoon

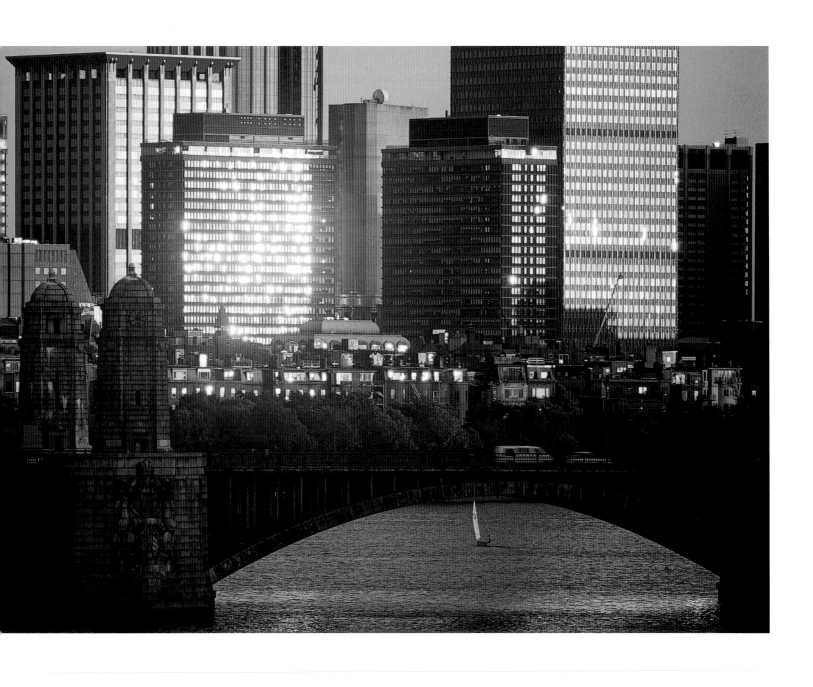

Back Bay and Longfellow Bridge   Lofts and warehouses, Summer Street

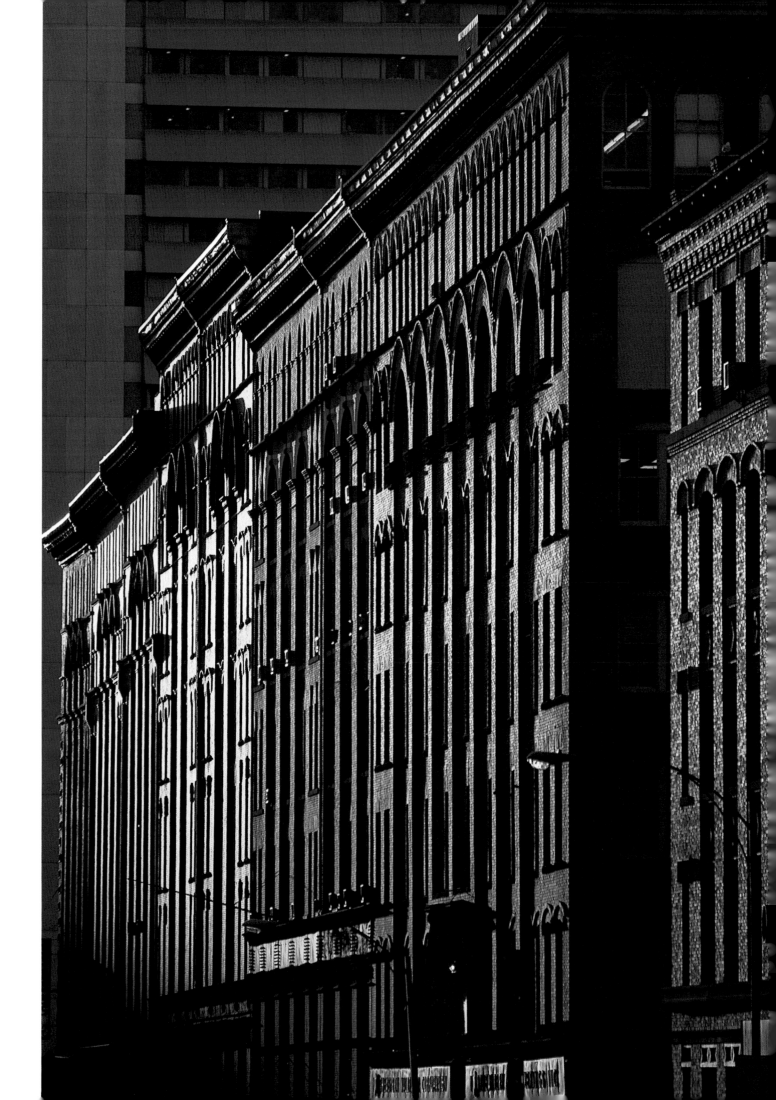

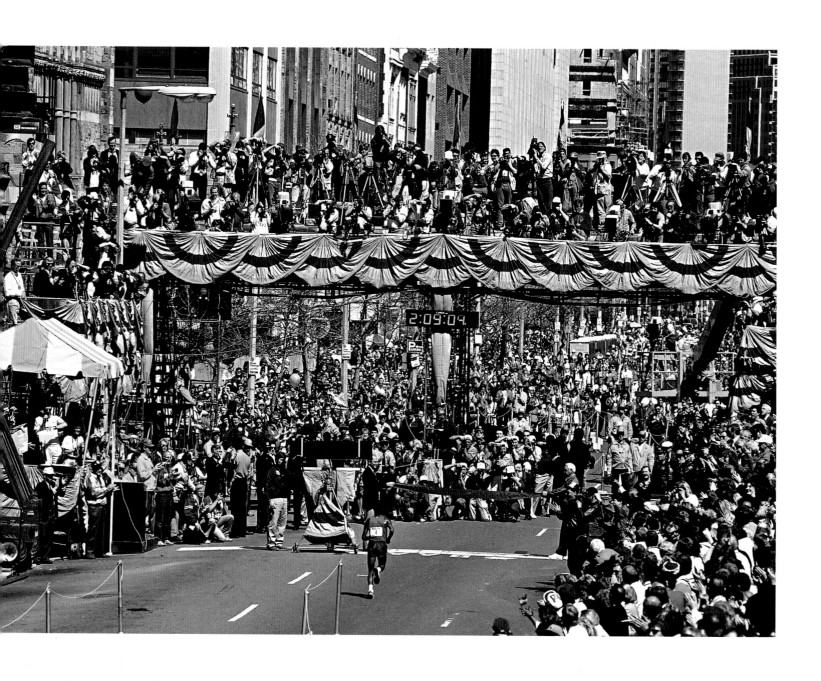

Marathon finish line, Boylston Street

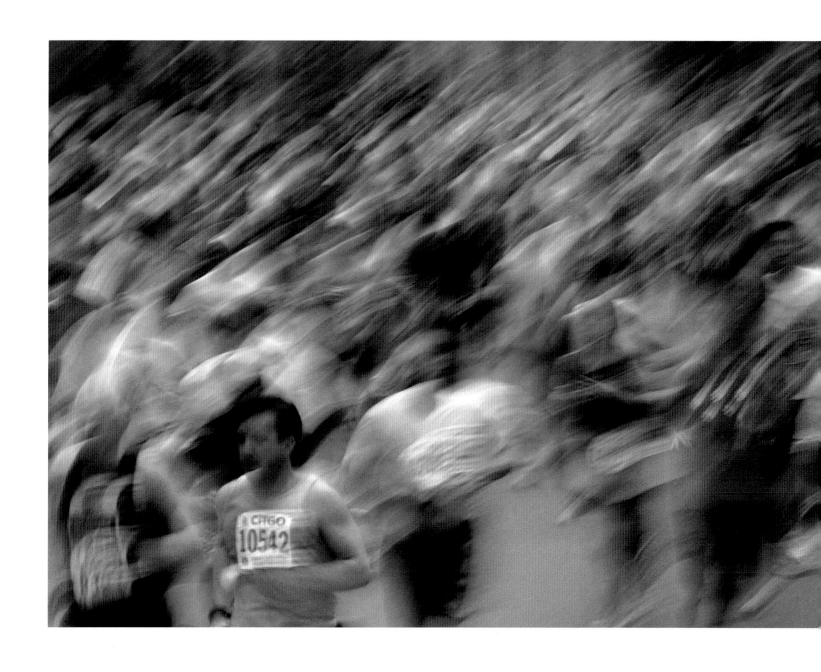

Boston Marathon turn at Gloucester Street

Overleaf: Downtown at dusk

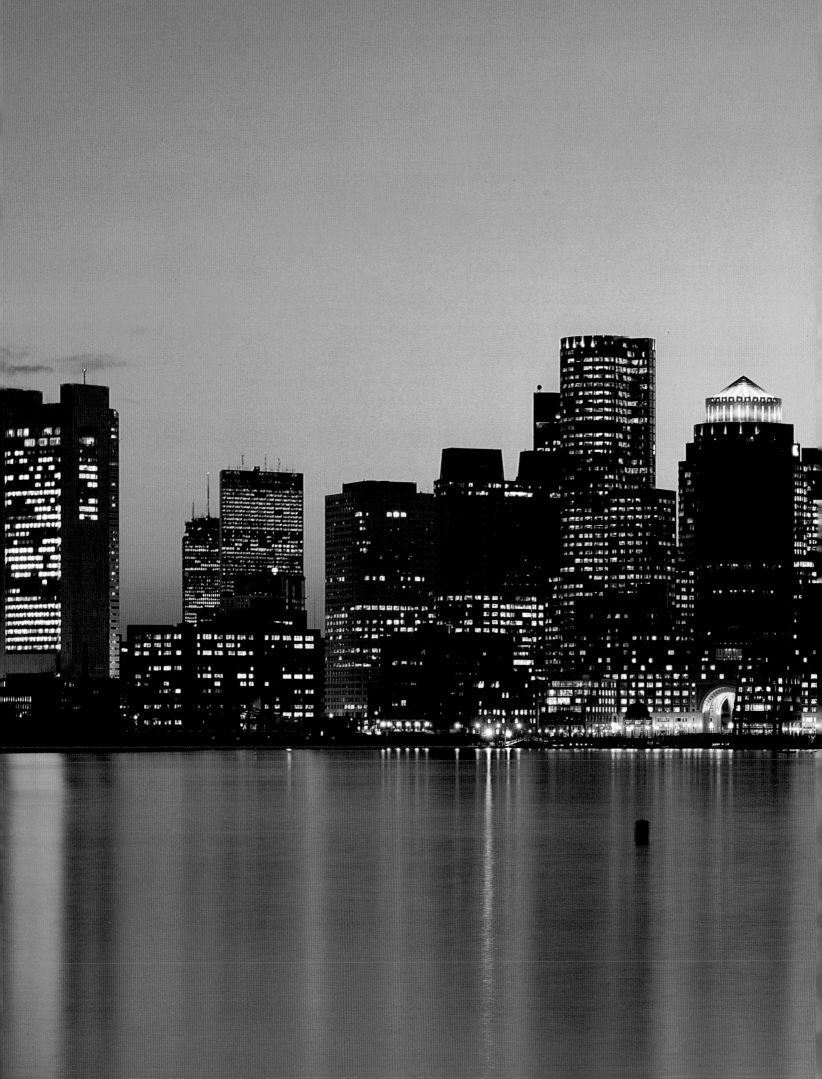

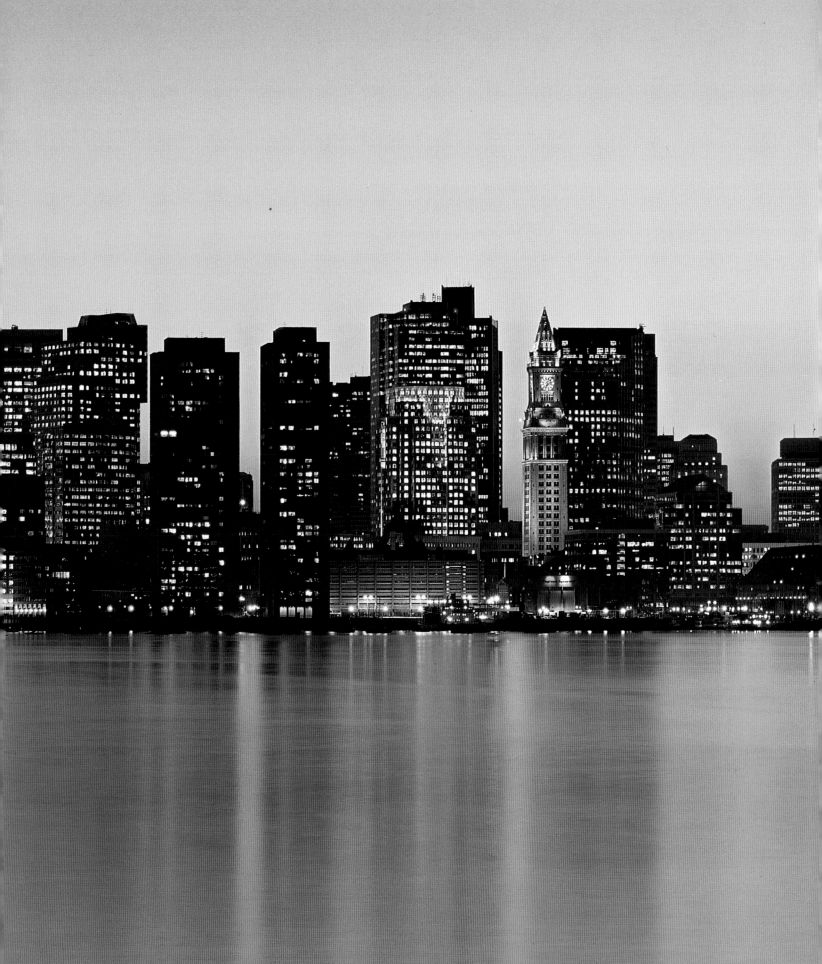

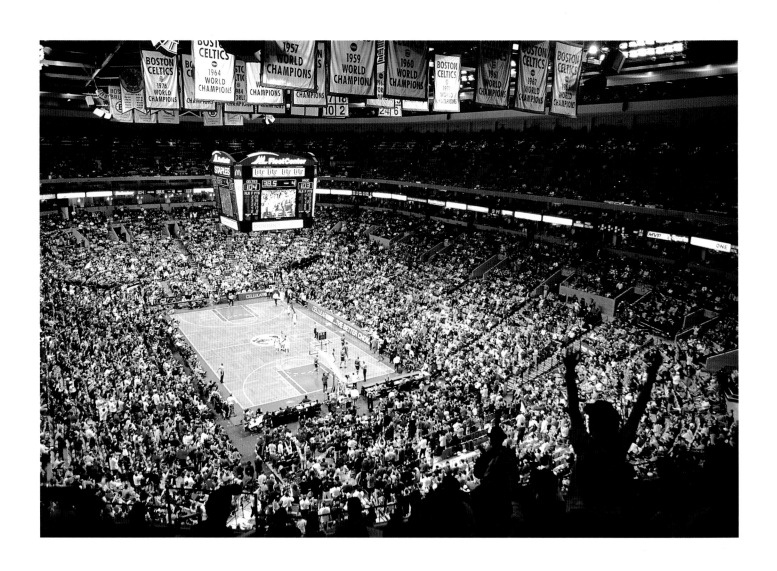

Boston Celtics overtime, Fleet Center

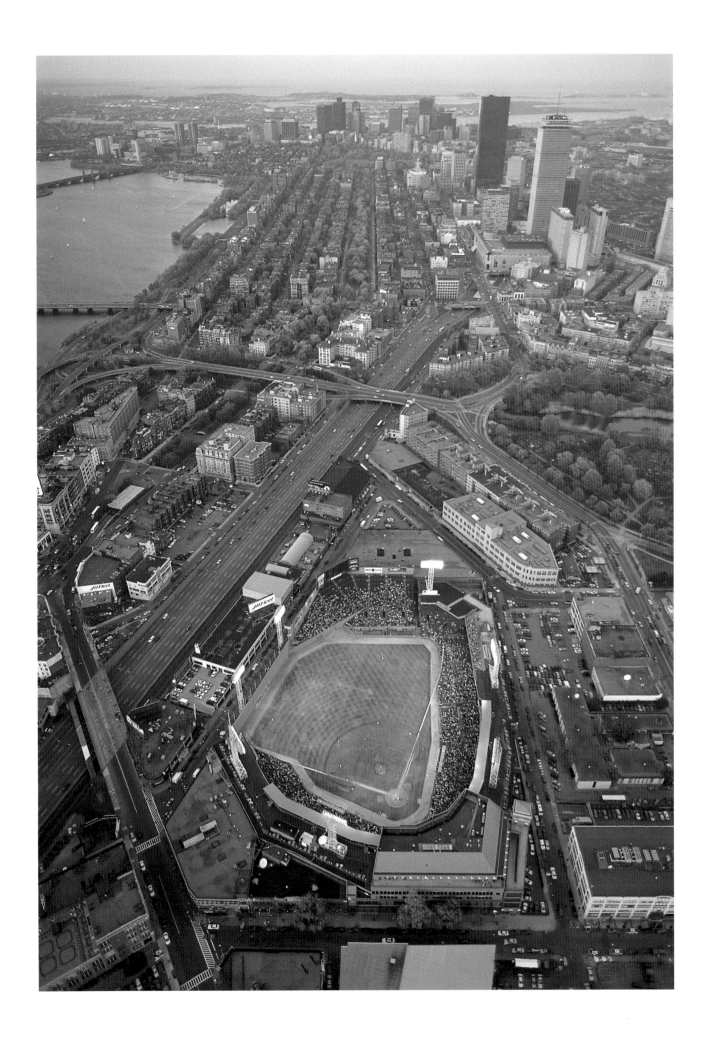

Boston Red Sox, Fenway Park

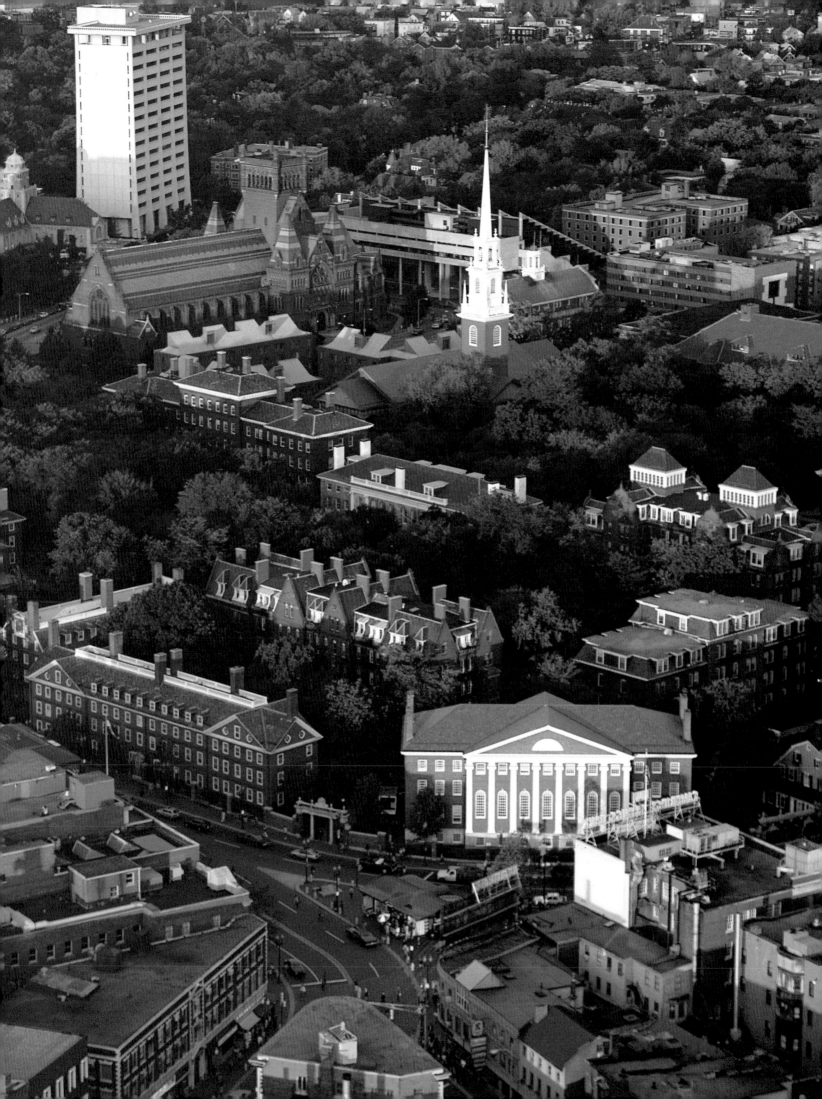

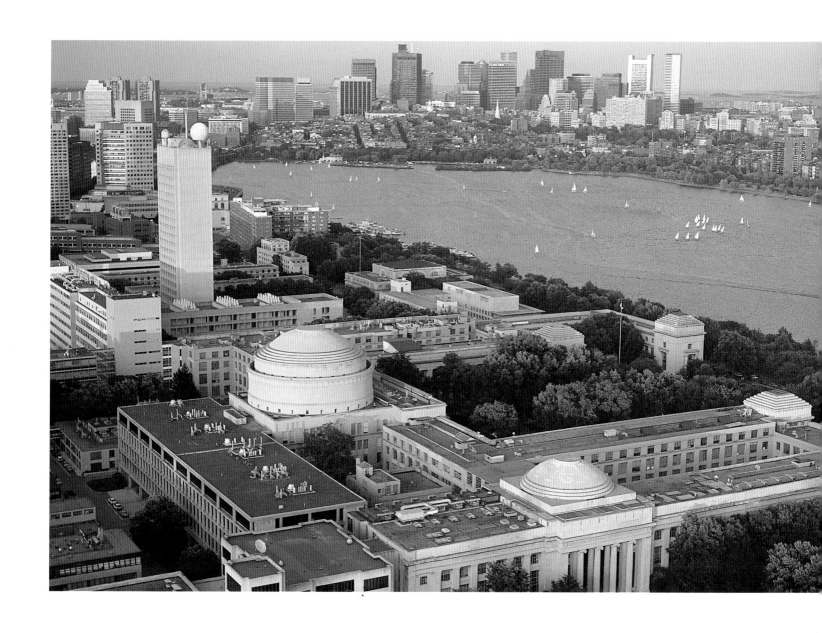

M.I.T. Campus, Cambridge to Boston

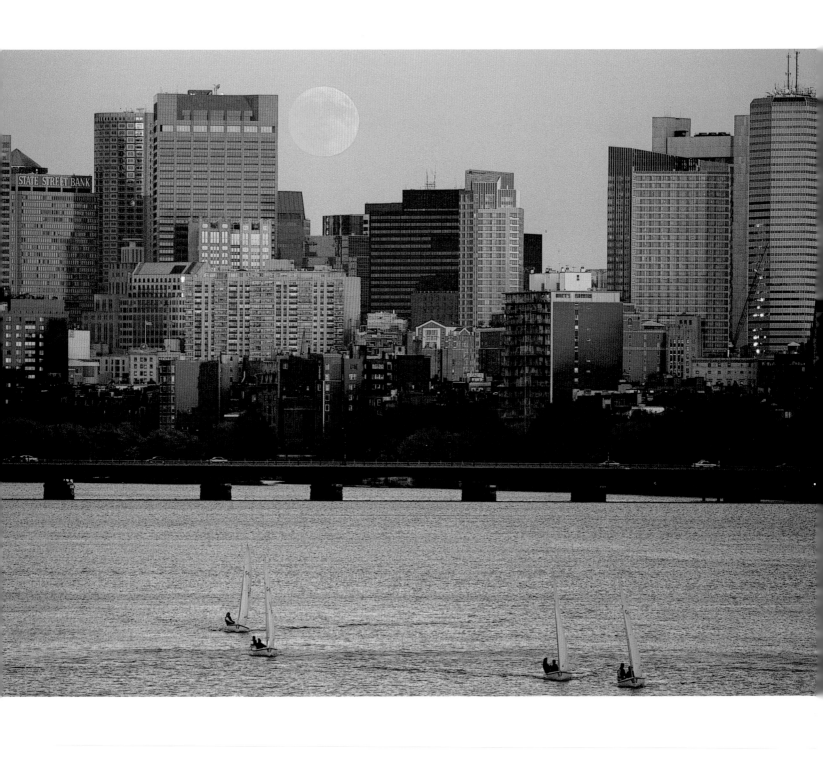

Moonrise, Charles River

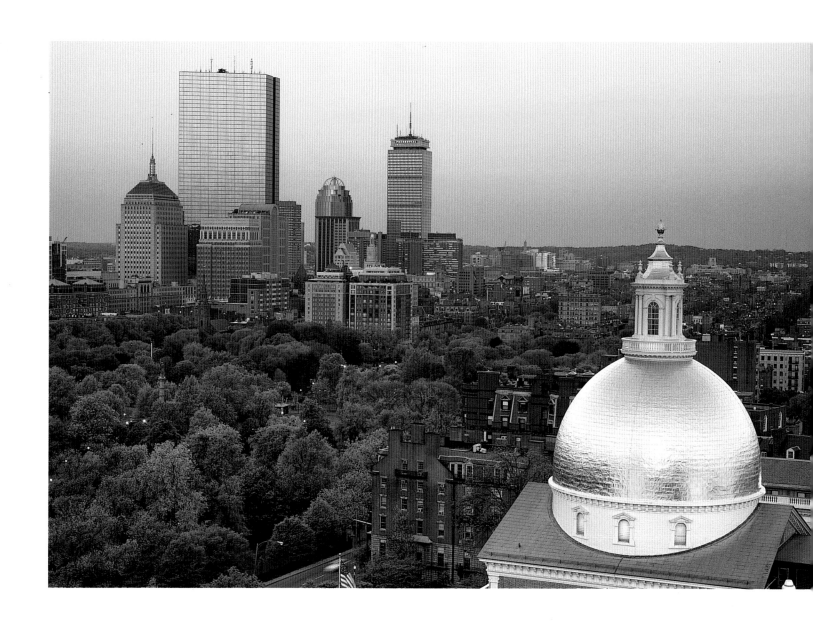

State House dome and Back Bay, sunrise

Overleaf: Skyline from Charlestown

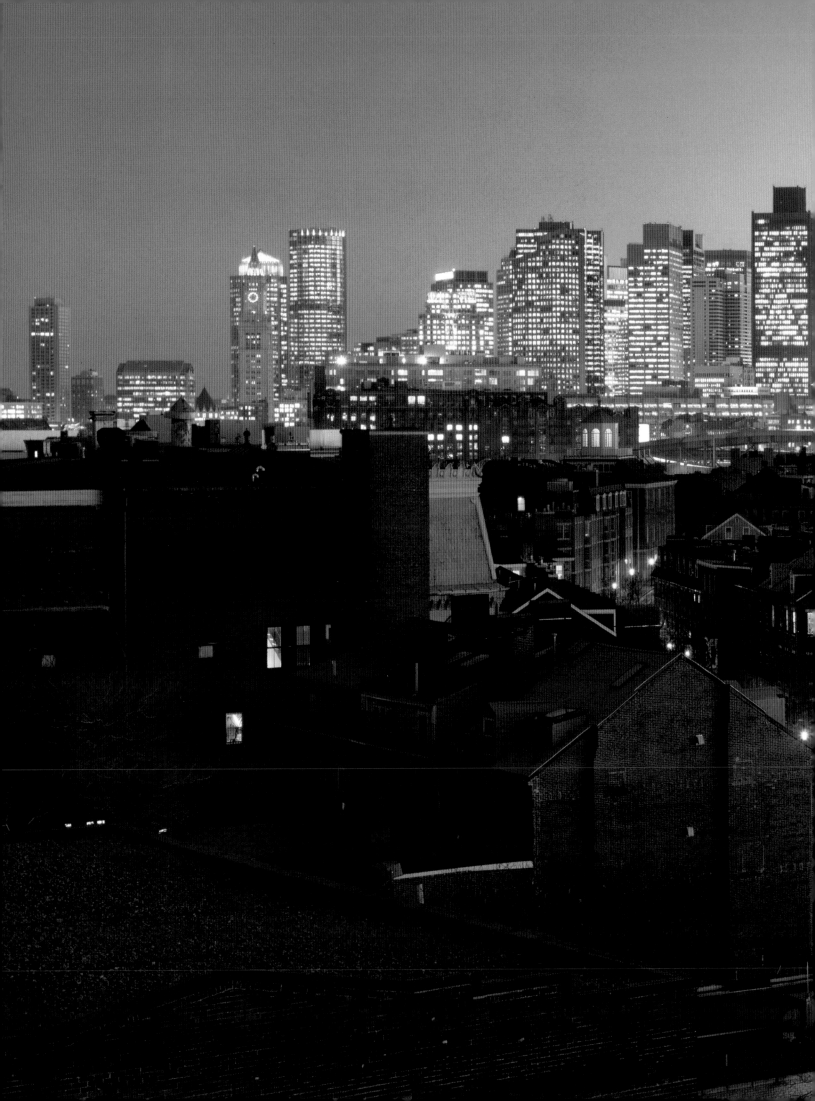

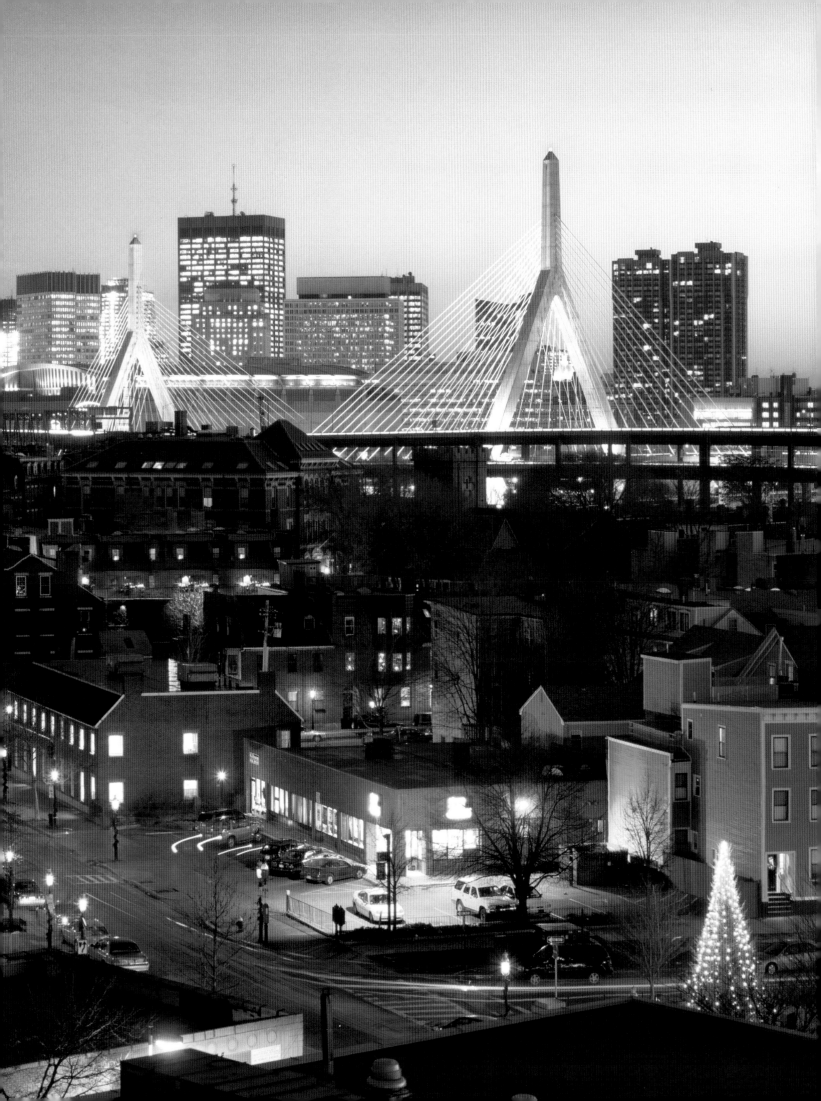

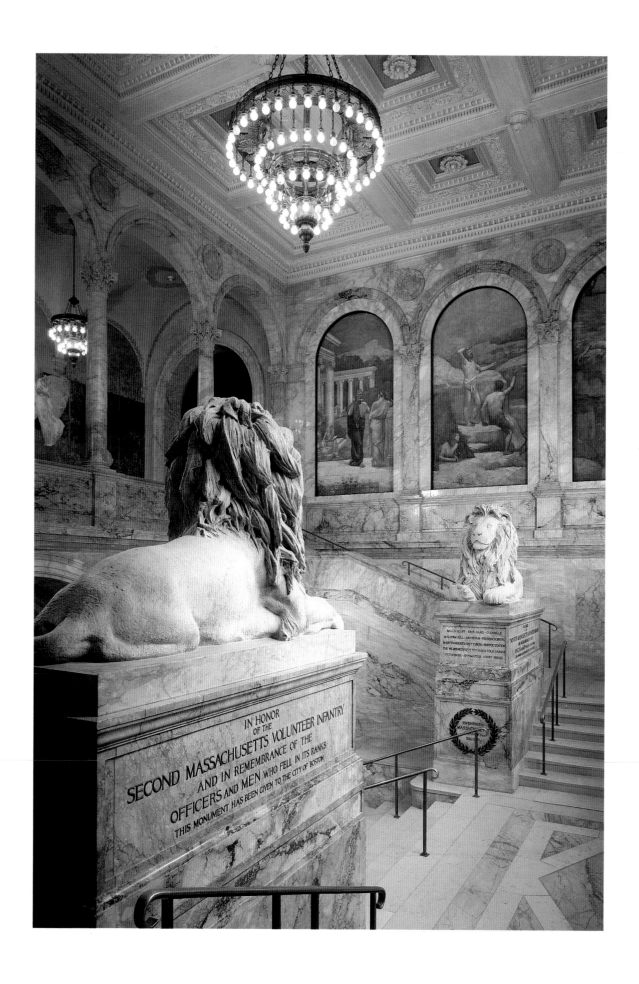

IN HONOR
OF THE
SECOND MASSACHUSETTS VOLUNTEER INFANTRY
AND IN REMEMBRANCE OF THE
OFFICERS AND MEN WHO FELL IN ITS RANKS·
THIS MONUMENT HAS BEEN GIVEN TO THE CITY OF BOSTON·

Public Library foyer

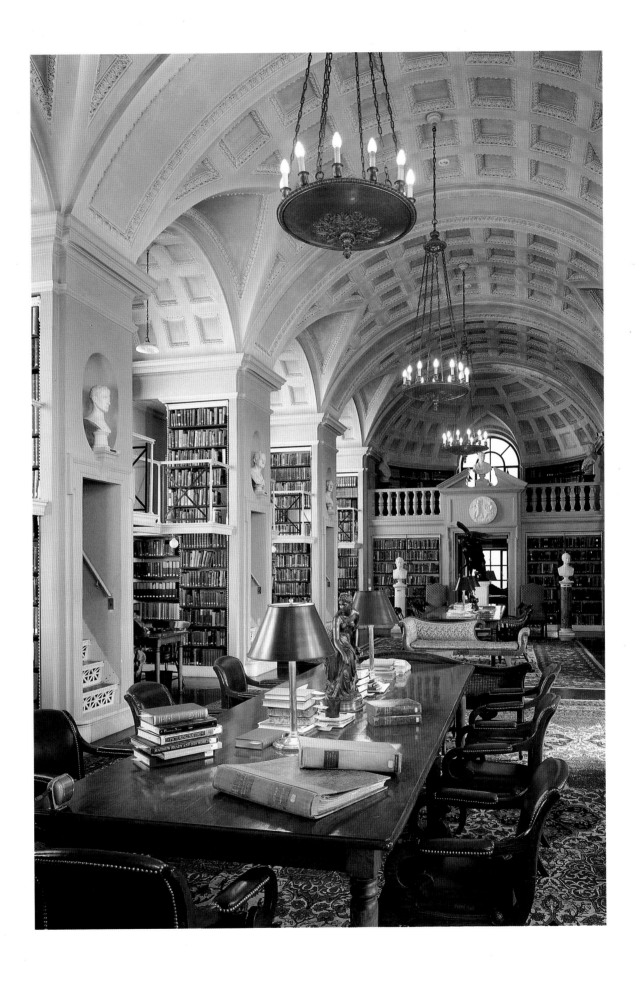

Athenaeum reading room   *Overleaf:* Acorn Street, Beacon Hill

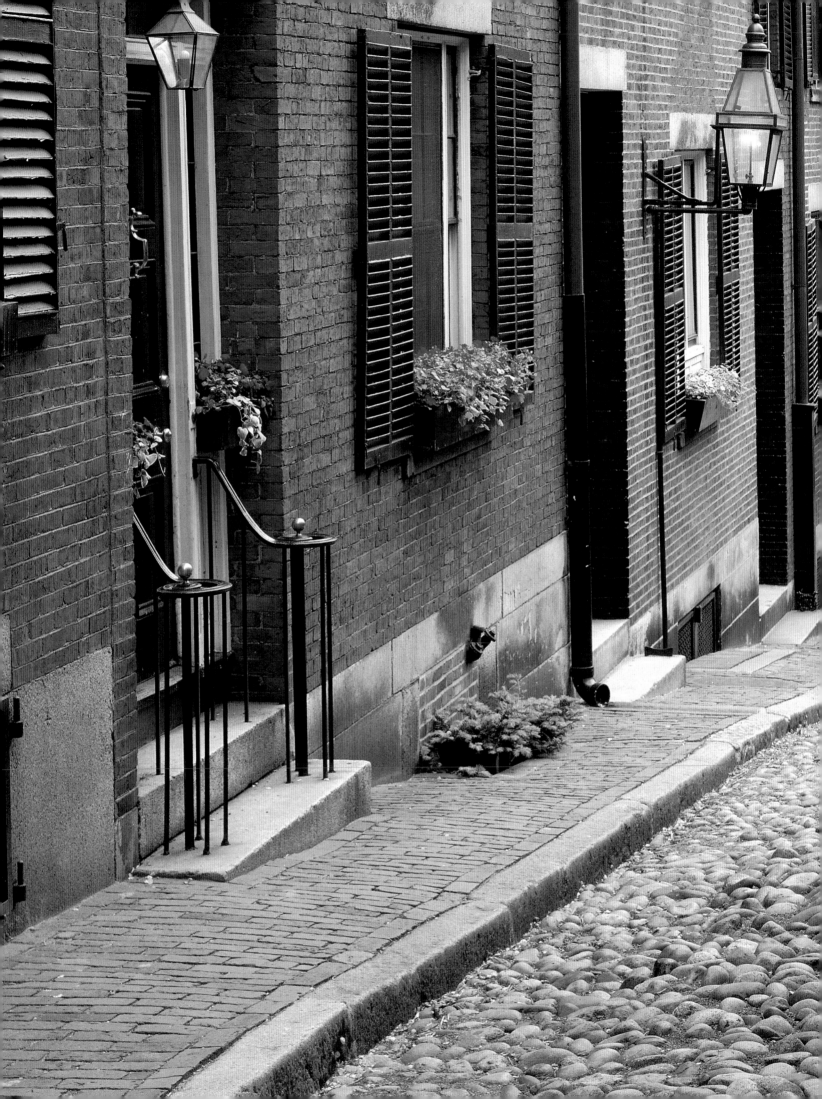

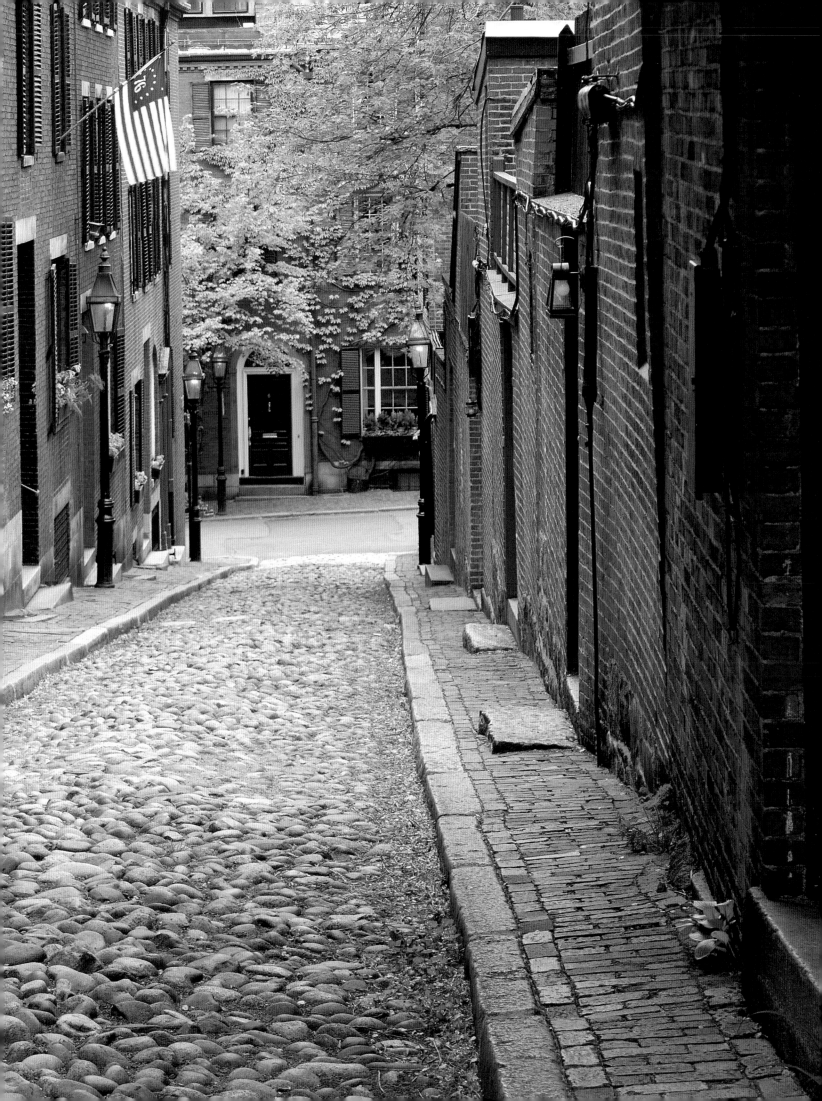

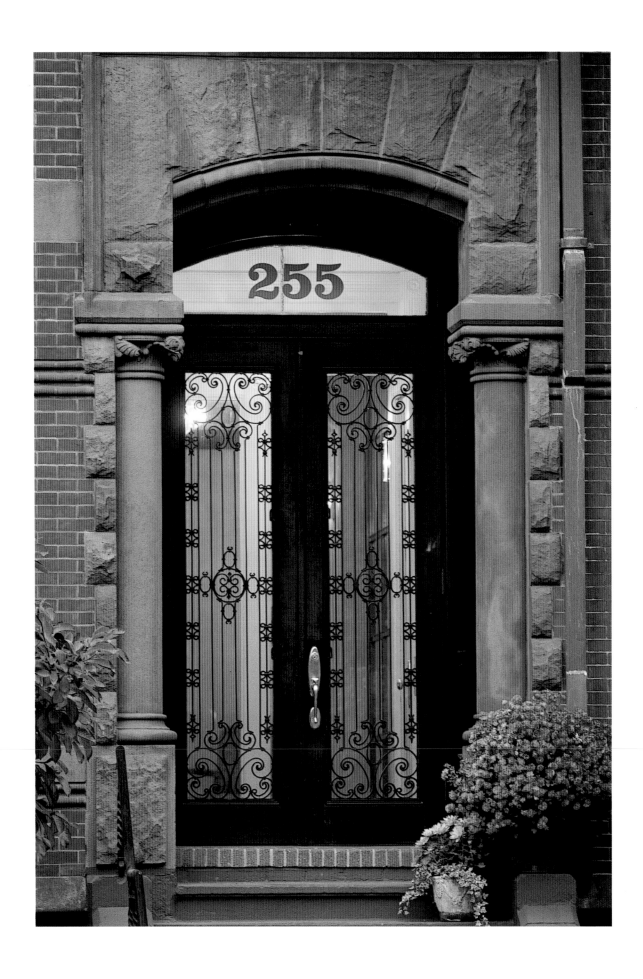

Commonwealth Avenue

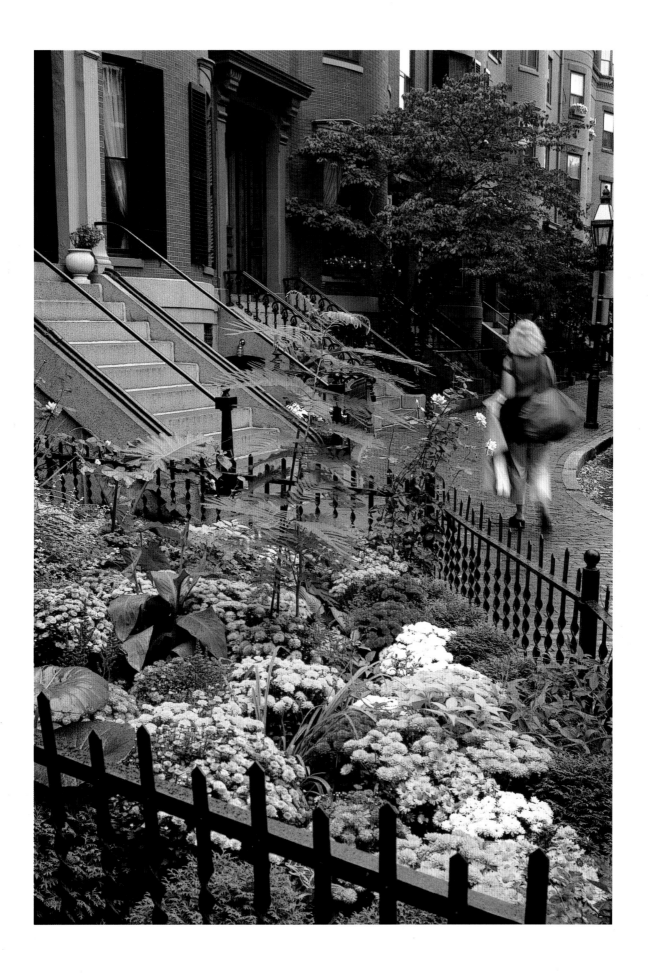

Union Park, South End   *Overleaf:* Harbor sunset, from Hull

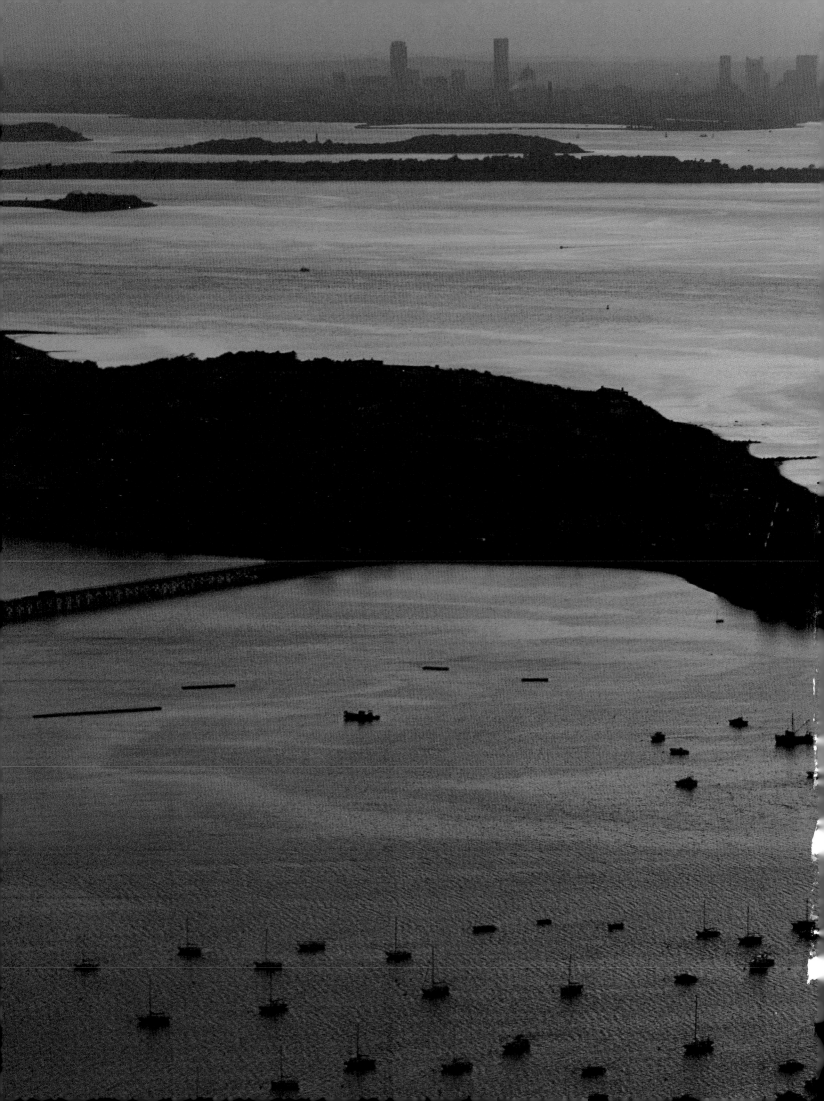

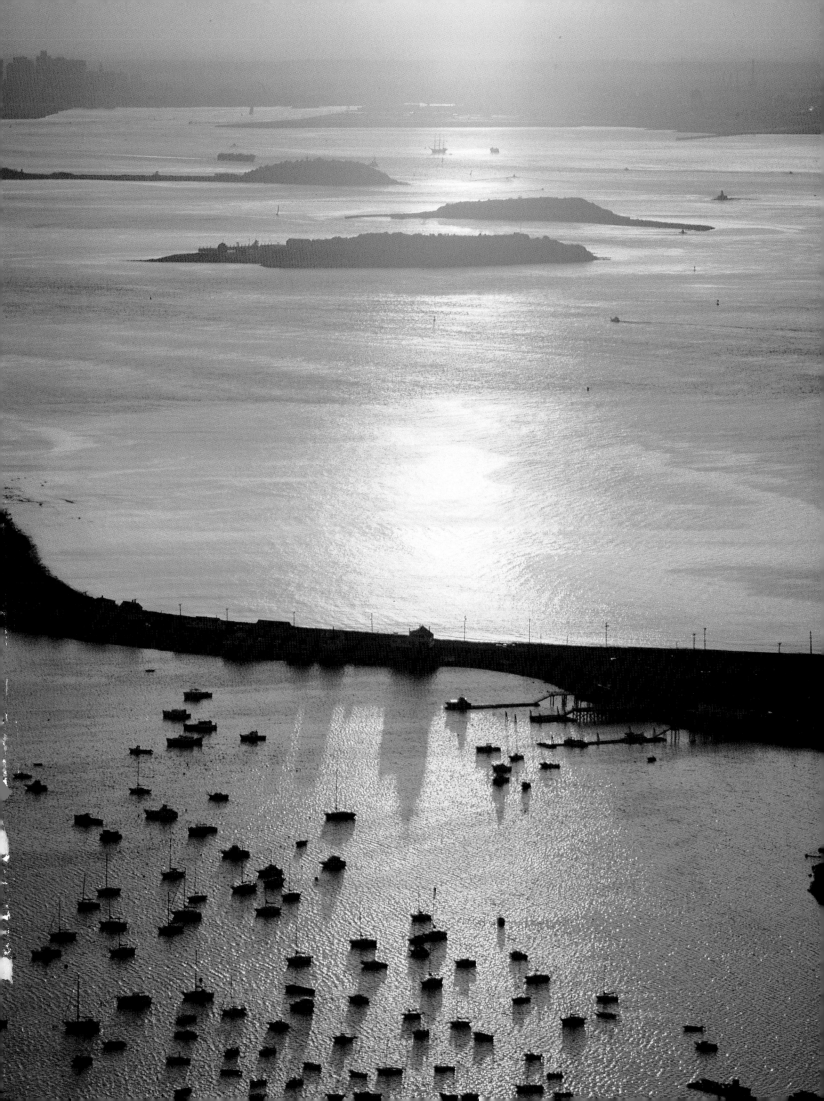

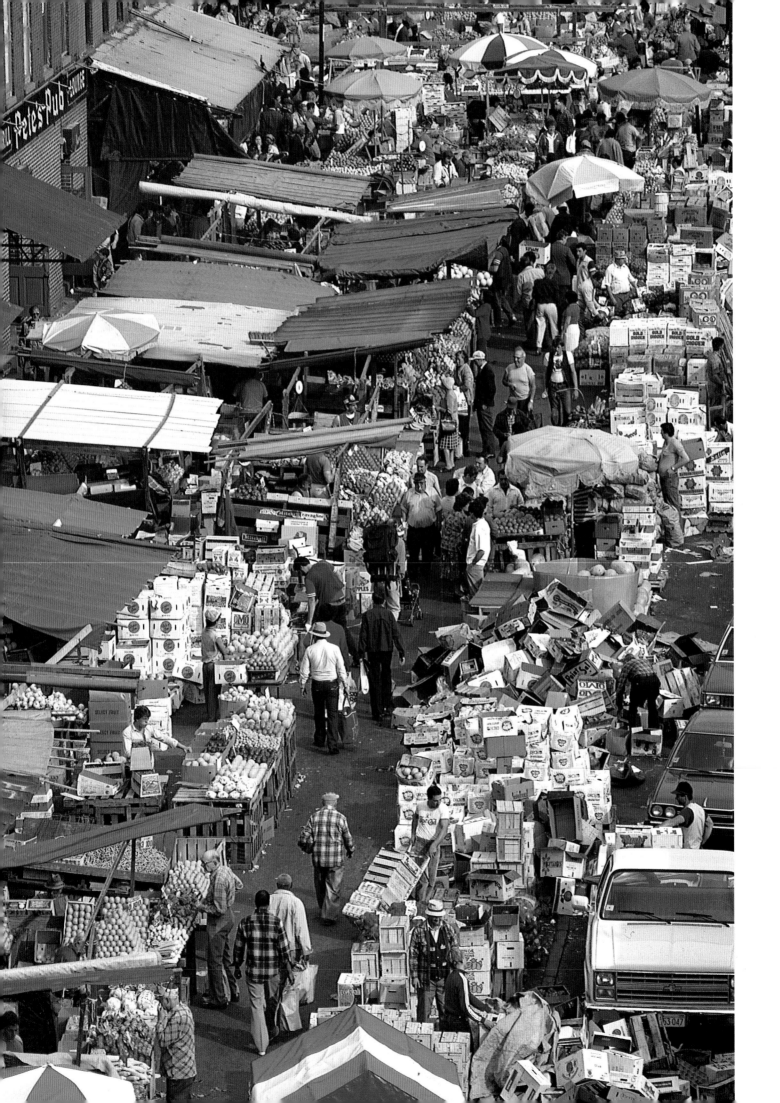

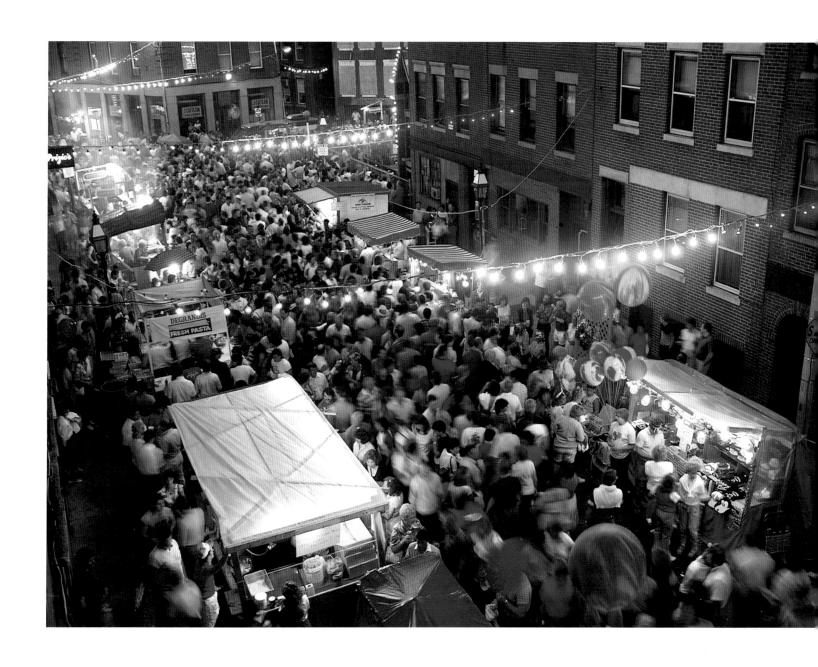

Saturday morning shopping, Haymarket Square   Festival of St. Anthony, Endicott Street, North End   *Overleaf:* The downtown waterfront

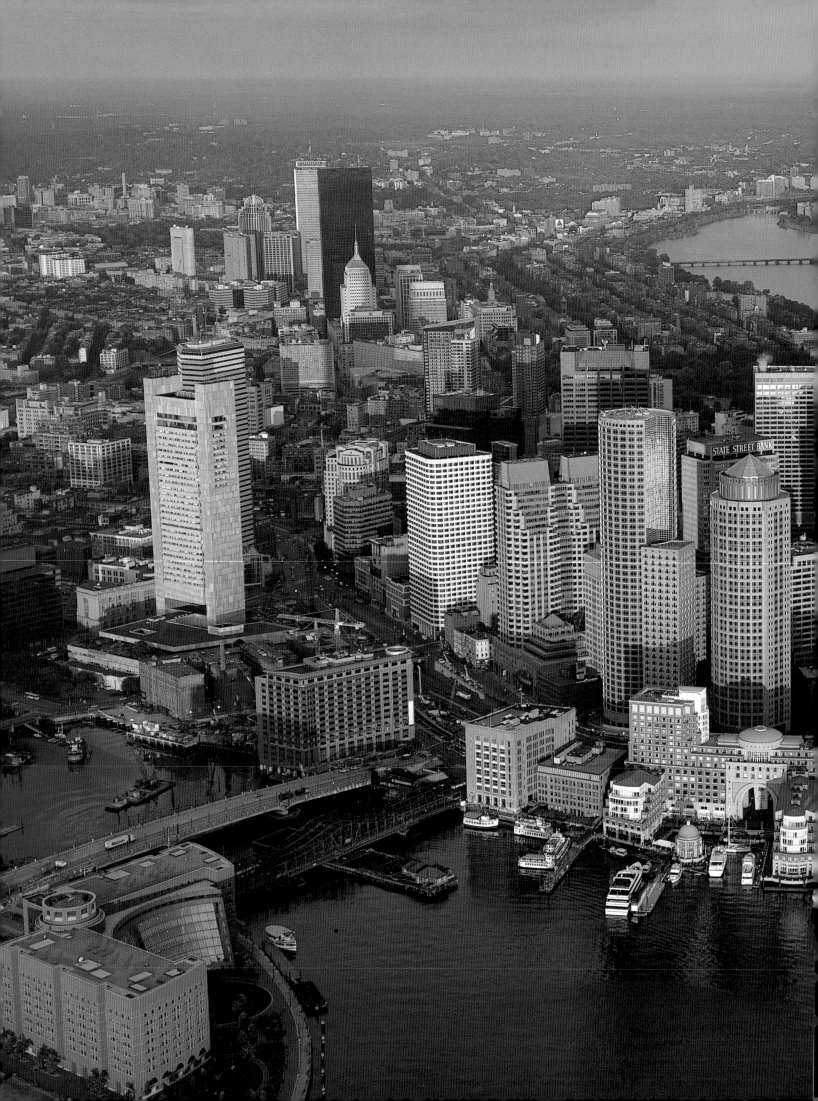

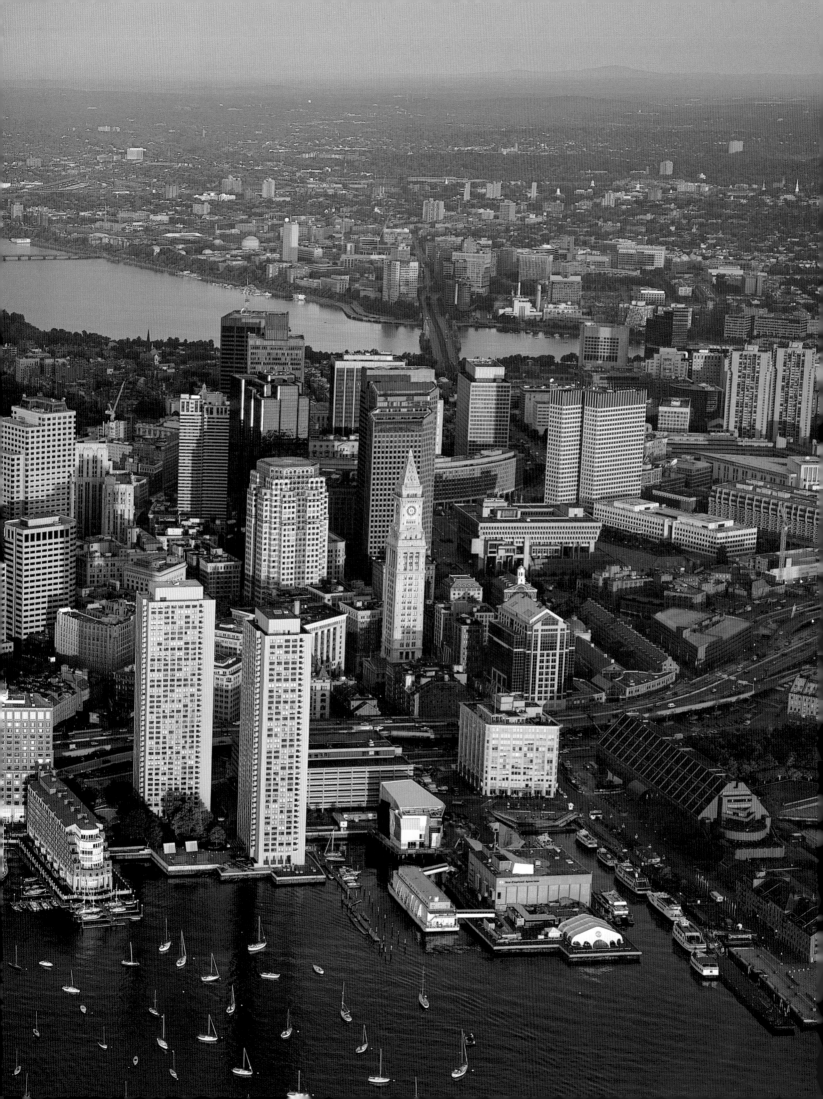

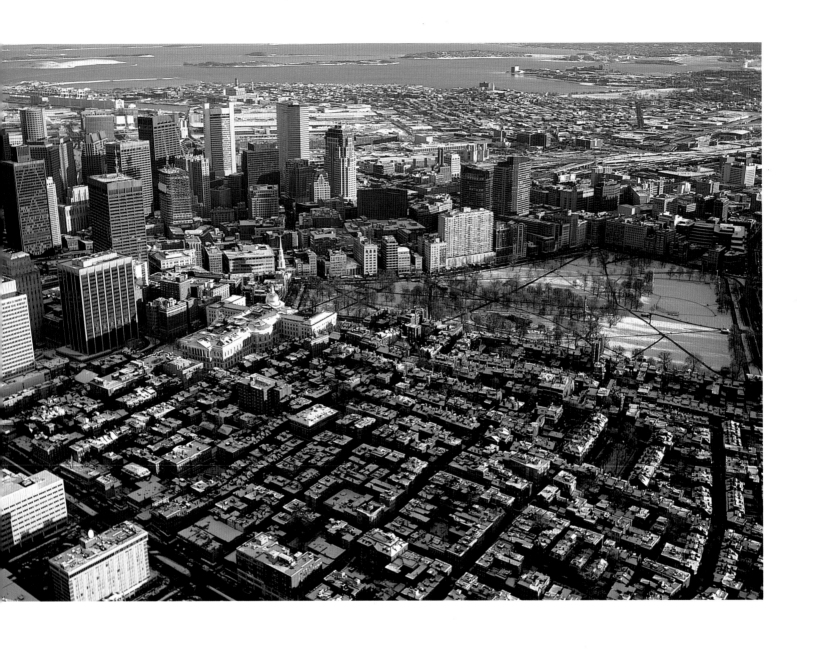

Beacon Hill

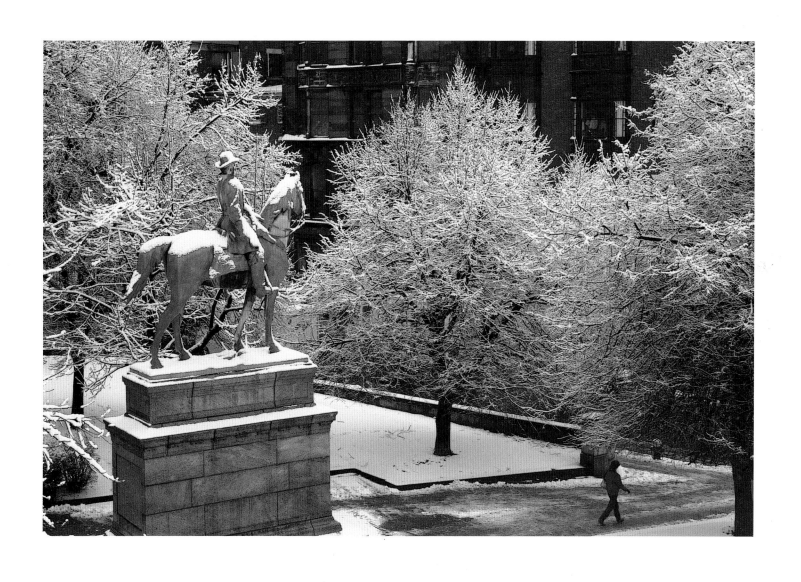

General Joseph Hooker statue, Beacon Street

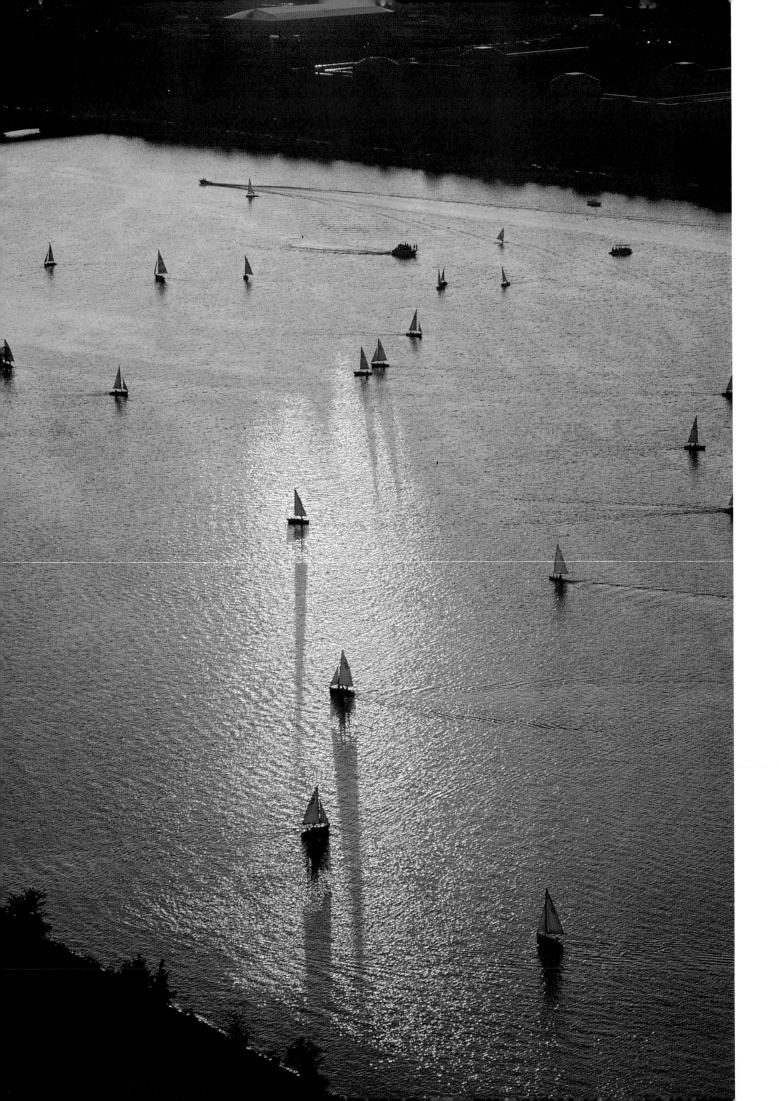

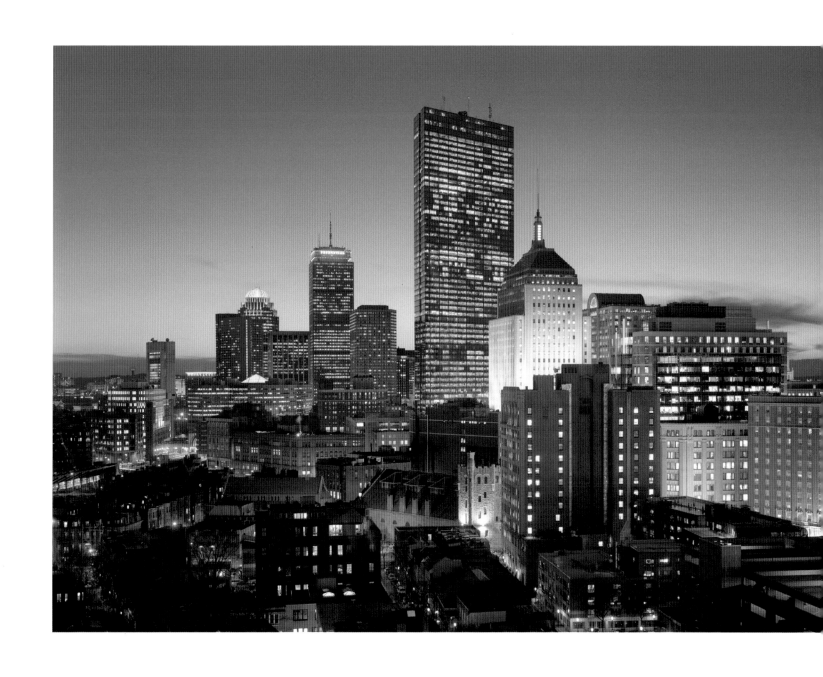

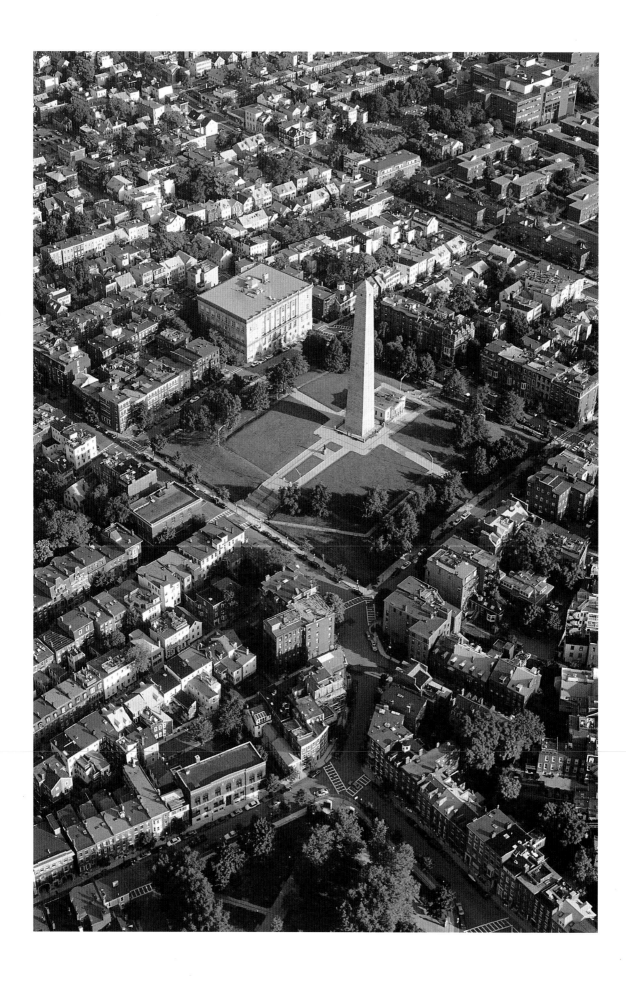

Bunker Hill, Charlestown

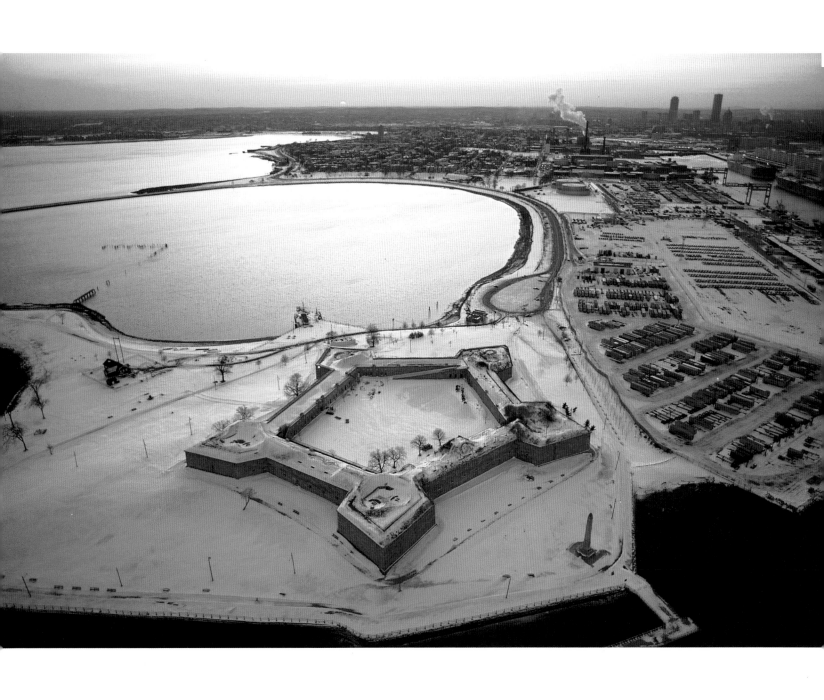

Fort Independence, Castle Island

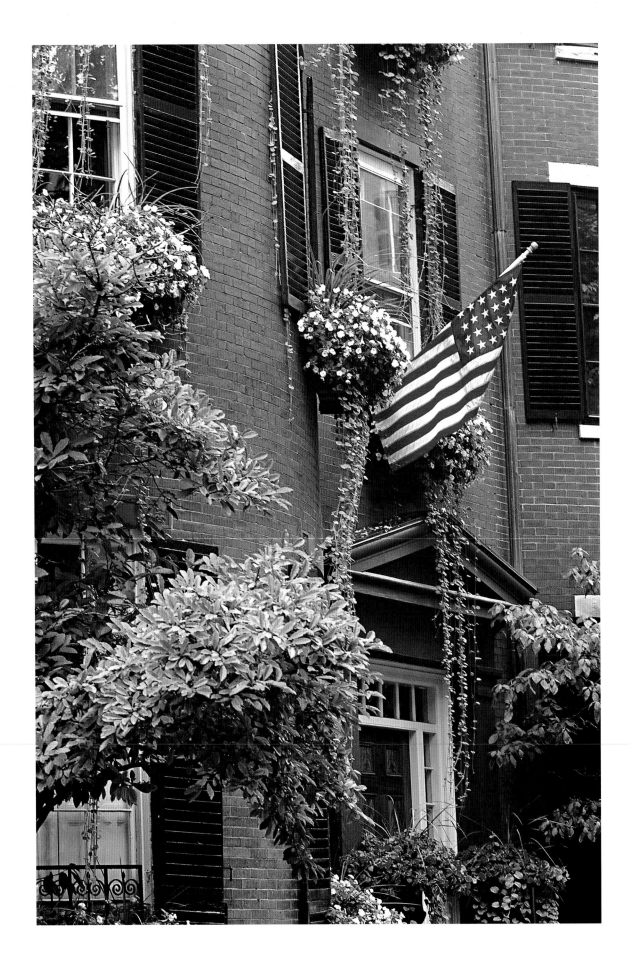

Louisburg Square

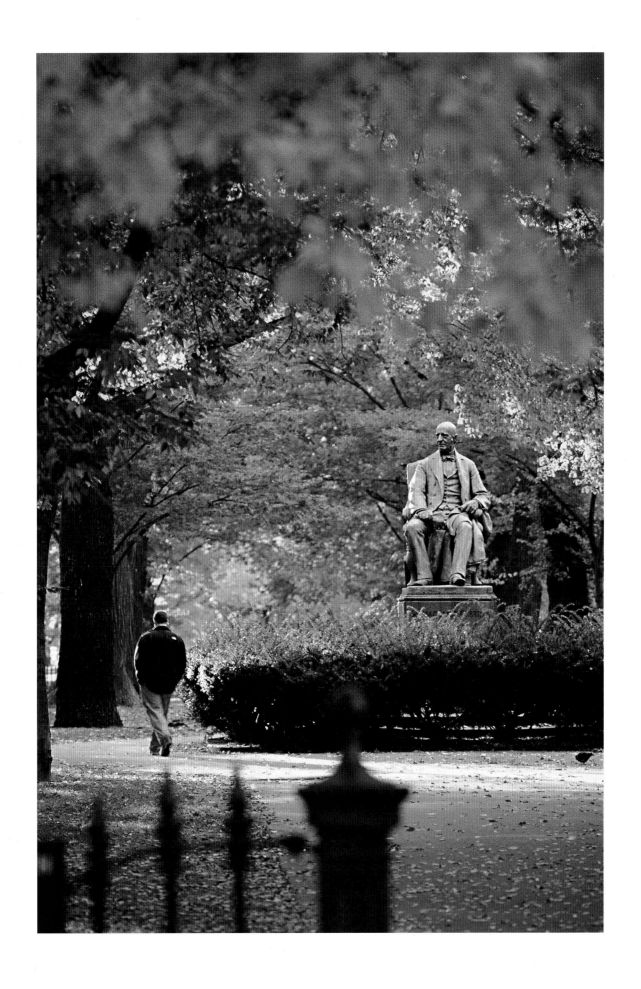

William Lloyd Garrison, Commonwealth Avenue

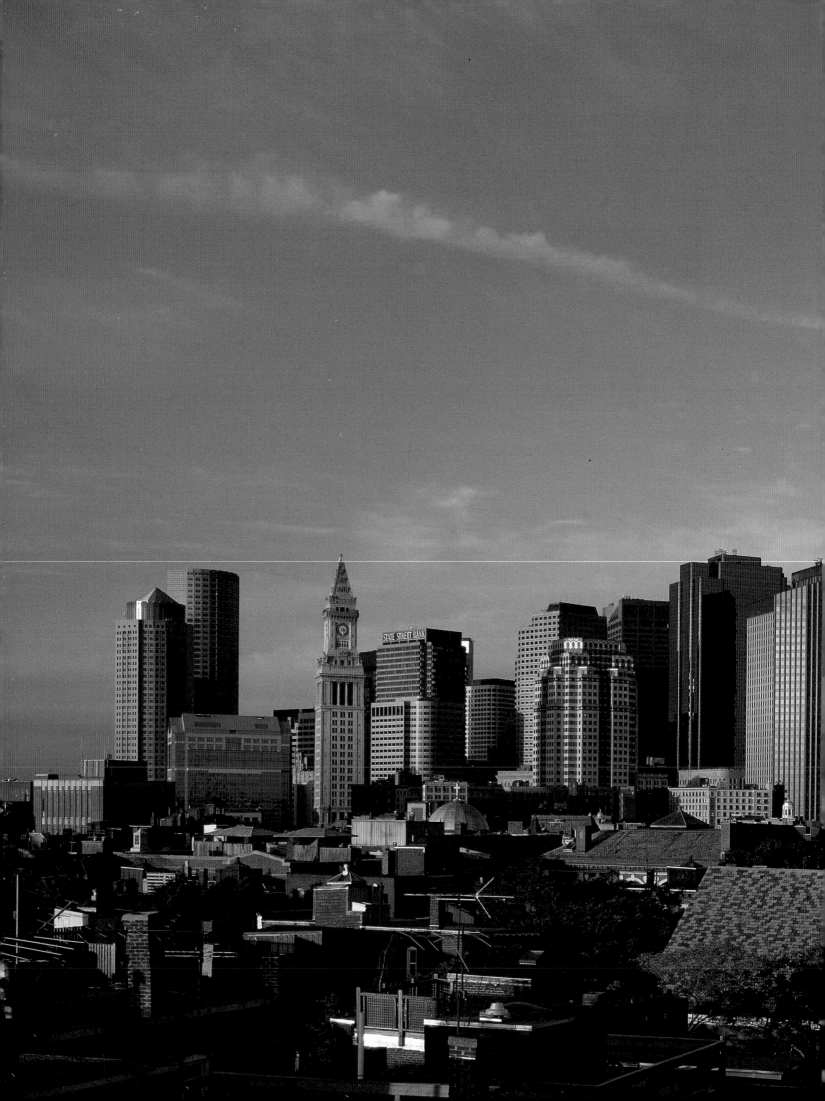

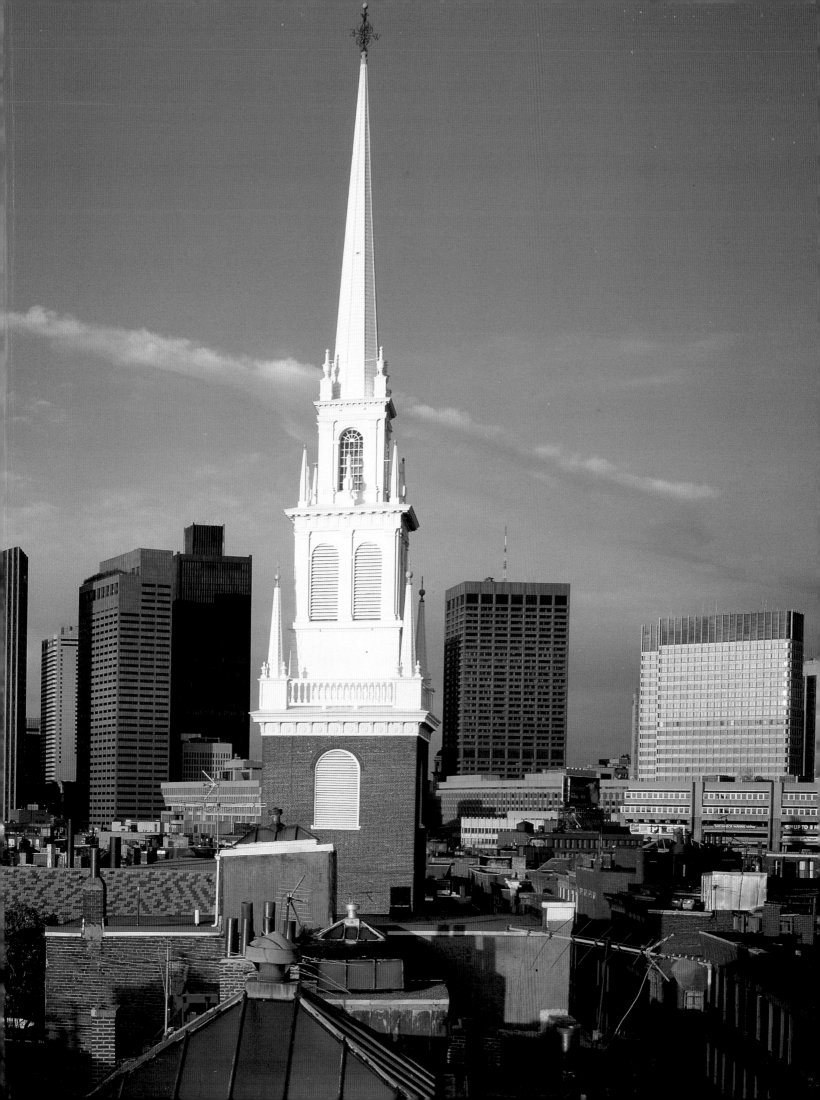

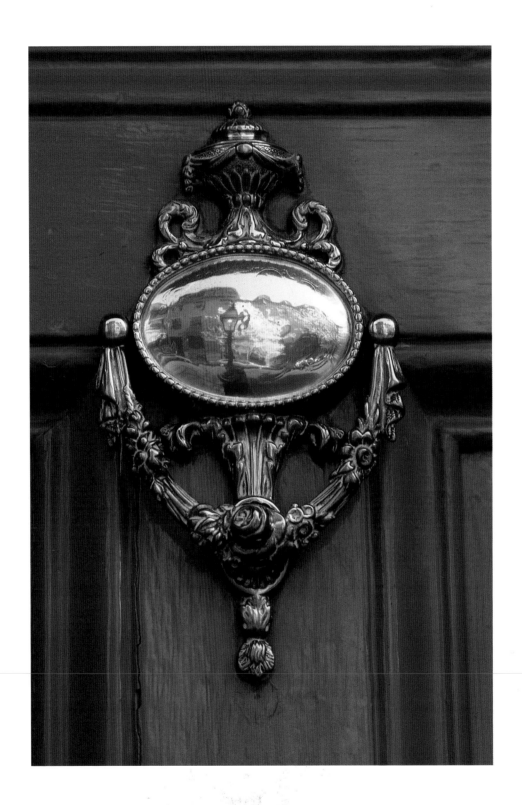

Beacon Hill